# Militarism

## Karl Liebknecht

DODO PRESS

MILITARISM

BY

KARL LIEBKNECHT

1917

# CONTENTS

I. THE NATURE AND SIGNIFICANCE OF MILITARISM

Origin and Foundation of Forms of Social Domination

Some Facts from the History of Militarism

II. CAPITALISTIC MILITARISM

Preliminary Remarks

"Militarism for Abroad," Navalism and Colonial Militarism. Possibilities of War and Disarmament

The Proletariat and War

Fundamental Features of "Militarism for Home" and its Purpose

Army Systems of Some Foreign Countries

Conclusions. Russia

III. MEANS AND EFFECTS OF MILITARISM

The Immediate Goal

Military Pedagogy. Training Soldiers

Semi-Official and Semi-Military Organization of the Civil Population

Other ways of influencing the Civilian Population in a Military Direction

Militarism as Machiavellism and as a Political Regulator

IV. CONCERNING SOME CARDINAL SINS OF MILITARISM

Maltreatment of Soldiers or Militarism as a Repentant, Yet Unreformed Sinner. Two Dilemmas

The Costs of Militarism or *La douloureuse*

The Army as a Weapon Against the Proletariat in the Economic Struggle.

Soldiers as the Competitors of Free Workers

The Army and Strike-Breaking

The Rule of the Sabre and Gun in Strikes

Italy

Austria-Hungary

Belgium

France

United States of America

Canada

Switzerland

Norway

Germany

Veterans' Associations and Strikes

The Army as a Weapon Against the Proletariat in the Political Struggle, or the Rule of the Cannon

Veterans' Associations in the Political Struggle

Militarism, a Menace to Peace

The Obstacles of the Proletarian Revolution

# KARL LIEBKNECHT

*"He sowed the seed that freedom men might reap."*

This book, which is now presented to American readers for the first time, has a unique history, and forms a vital part of Liebknecht's long struggle against militarism. In September, 1906, Dr. Karl Liebknecht, the author, delivered a lecture on "Militarism" at a conference of young people Germany. The revised lecture was published in book form and the most important portions appear in the following pages. For some time, the German authorities paid little heed to it, and it was not until April 23, 1907, that the book was confiscated and the author charged with treason.

Liebknecht's trial began on the ninth of October, 1907, and lasted three days. The defendant was found guilty and sentenced to a year and a half of imprisonment. In sentencing him, the Imperial Court declared that Liebknecht aimed at the abolition of the standing army, and that this army was an integral part of the nation's constitution. In one statement, made in the latter part of his lecture, he had theorized concerning the possible future activities of the troops in behalf of the coming revolution, asserting that these activities might be regarded as the logical result of the demoralization of the military spirit. From this statement, which was a purely theoretical hypothesis, the Imperial Court concluded that Liebknecht's intention was to injure the morale of the army. The destruction of this morale, it declared, could be brought about only by forcible means, and the use of such means was but the first step in the destruction of the constitution. The court paid absolutely no attention to the statement of the author that only lawful means should be used in bringing about the change, and that no agitation should be conducted which would incite the soldiers directly or indirectly to disobedience. The Socialist Party, Liebknecht had maintained, as in the past, should energetically defend the private soldiers and the non-commissioned officers, should represent their material and professional interests in the press and in parliament and should endeavor tactfully to win the sympathies of these circles. In such remarks a German Imperial Court discovered high treason!

The trial was one of the most sensational ever held in Europe. The Kaiser, it was afterwards learned, was *kept constantly in touch with the progress of the trial by a special wire.* The attorney general urged the accused to plead guilty and promised, if this were done, to ask the court for clemency. To this plea, Liebknecht quickly retorted, "I take entire responsibility for every word~I have written." On the second day of the trial, the defendant declared in open court that he was convinced that a verdict of guilty had already been decided on. His address to the judges was one of the clearest, most incisive and boldest attacks ever made against German militarism.

"The aim of my life," he declared, "is the overthrow of monarchy, as well as the emancipation of the exploited working class from political and economic bondage. As my father, who appeared before this court exactly thirty-five years ago to defend himself against the charge of treason; was ultimately pronounced victor, so I believe the day not far distant when the principles which I represent will be recognized as patriotic, as honorable, as true."

Liebknecht's courageous stand on this occasion was rewarded by a sentence of a year and a half in a military prison, as before stated. As a sharp rebuke to this sentence, the working people of Berlin promptly nominated and elected him, while still in prison, as their representative for the Prussian Landtag. It was in the Landtag that Liebknecht started his real campaign against Prussian militarism. His attacks against the system were bitter. Time without number he was called to order by the chair; frequently he was removed from the floor of the chamber.

He represented the working people of Berlin, as well, in the Common Council, and in 1912, the citizens of Potsdam-Spandau who were employed for the most part in government ammunition works, selected him as their representative in the Reichstag. I saw Liebknecht during the great campaign preceding his election. He described the methods employed by the government to defeat him. The government endeavored to show that he was anti-patriotic, because he had failed to uphold its hands in the Morocco affair. To this the workers gave a deaf ear. The next move was an attempt to terrorize the state employees. The authorities even went so far as to make a ruling prohibiting them from voting for him on the ground that he was an enemy of the state. However, the dissatisfaction with the government was great. The campaign of intimidation failed and Liebknecht was elected by an overwhelming vote, to the intense joy of those who knew and loved him.

I saw the surging crowd before the office of the Berlin *Vorwarts* the night of the election, and heard the wild applause when announcement of his election was made. A young workingman exclaimed to those who were around him:"The new voice of freedom will be heard from now on in the Reichstag." The words were prophetic. This body never heard stronger protests against the domination of the civil mind by the military than those which this new apostle uttered. He issued his invectives against the armament trust, and showed its corrupting influence over government officials and press. He gave to the public the story of a late Prussian general, who lived by borrowing a not infrequent habit of these officers and by trading in government medals and positions and honorary titles. The general had been in the good graces of the Kaiser, and the story did little to increase the prestige of the latter or of the military caste. The man about to be selected by the Kaiser as war secretary was exposed by the anti-militarist member of Parliament as an ordinary swindler and the honesty of the military group was thereby further brought into question.

Liebknecht also raised his voice in behalf of a German Republic at a time when those who now declare that the only way to end the war is by making Germany a republic, supported and encouraged the German monarchy. On one memorable occasion, in a debate in the Prussian Landtag over the building of the new opera house, Liebknecht took the floor and declared: "The opera house for which we are asked to vote the necessary funds, should last for many generations. We trust that it will last long after it has lost its character as a Royal Opera House."

This daring statement brought upon his head scathing denunciations from the majority of the members, who were unable to imagine how one could dare suggest a republic in a Prussian parliament. And this pronouncement was issued long before kings and presidents dreamed of fighting to make the world safe for democracy, for humanity.

When the European war broke out, a meeting was called of the Social-Democratic members of the Reichstag, for the purpose of deciding what stand the party should take on the war. Karl Kautsky, the theoretical leader of Socialism, was also invited. It was, perhaps, the stormiest meeting ever held by that group. The majority contended that this was a war of defense; that Germany was attacked by Russia; that, although there was little liberty in Germany, there was still less in Russia, and that Socialists should, therefore, vote for the war budget. Furthermore, some argued, by this action it will be possible for Socialists to secure further rights from the government. Should they take the opposite course, the funds of the labor unions will be confiscated, and the Socialist press and movement, built up through long years of painful endeavor, will be destroyed. Finally, as Socialists do not constitute the majority, the war budget will, in any case, be passed whether they support it or not.

A second group, represented by Kautsky, advised that the party abstain from voting altogether. A vote against the war budget might leave the country defenseless. The Socialist, it was understood, would defend the country in case of attack, especially should such attack come from such a country as Russia. Germany, this group believed, was then being attacked by the forces of the Czar. By taking the middle-of-the road position, and voting neither for nor against the budget, the Socialist would not be voting against the defence of his country, and on the other hand, would not be assuming responsibility for all of the acts committed by his government prior to the war. Since then, it may be said in passing, Kautsky has taken a more militant position against the war.

The third group was represented by Liebknecht. "This war," argued Liebknecht and his followers, "is an imperialist war for-domination of world markets, and for the benefit of bankers and manufacturers. It is also a war tending to destroy' the growing labor movement. It is not a war of' defense. It is therefore our plain duty to vote against the war budget."

The first position won out, and according to the rules governing the organization of the group, the minority had to bow to the decision of the majority. It was for this reason that the entire Social Democratic delegation voted for the war budget at the first open meeting of the Reichstag after the outbreak of the war. At the second session in December Liebknecht was the only man who dared to stand up in the Reichstag. against the decision of all parties and vote against the budget.

He not only cast his vote, but he also dared- to state in an open meeting of the Reichstag to a Germany then apparently victorious, that the Germans were the aggressors in the war, and that it was an imperialistic war provoked by his country and Austria. He protested against the violation of Belgium and Luxembourg; against the military dictatorship; against Prussian and German autocracy. Whether one agrees or disagrees with his position, one cannot but admit the courageous character of the act, which is bound to be recorded as one of the most heroic of the world drama.

On May. 1, 1916, Liebknecht participated in a May Day Peace demonstration in Berlin. It was on this occasion that he delivered the peace address which brought- to him an imprisonment of four years and one month of hard labor.

"We Germans in Prussia," he declared, "have three cardinal rights: the right to be soldiers, to pay taxes, to keep our tongues between our teeth.

"Poverty and misery, need and starvation, are ruling in Germany. Belgium, Poland and Serbia, whose blood the vampire of imperialism is sucking, resemble vast cemeteries2 The entire world, the much praised European civilization, is falling into ruin through the anarchy which has been let loose by the world war.

"Those who profit from the war desire war with America. To-morrow, perhaps, they may order us to aim weapons against new groups of our brothers, against our fellow workers in America. Consider well the fact: as long as the German people do not rise and enforce their own will, the assassination of the people will continue. Let thousands of voices shout: 'Down with the shameless extermination of nations! Down with those who are responsible for these crimes !' "

Immediately after his anti-war address, Liebknecht was arrested. He claimed parliamentary immunity, but this claim was not allowed. While in prison awaiting trial, he sent two letters to the military court, containing the reasons why he opposed the German government, militarism and the war. These letters are powerful indictments against these institutions as well as against international capitalism the breeder of war.

"The cry of down with the war" is meant to give voice to the fact that I thoroughly condemn and oppose the present war because of its historical nature; because of its general social causes; the particular way in which it was brought about, the manner in which it is conducted and the object for which it is fought. I oppose it also in the belief that it is the duty of every representative of the proletariat to take part in the international class struggle for the purpose of putting an end thereto. As a Socialist, I am a thorough-going opponent of the existing military system as well as of this war. I have always supported with all my power the battle against militarism. Its overthrow is a particularly important task for the working class of all countries to perform; in fact, it is a matter of life and death to them.

"In partnership with the Austrian government," he declared, "it [the German government] plotted to bring about this war and thus burdened itself with the principal responsibility for its immediate outbreak. It began the war by misleading the masses of people, and even by misleading the Reichstag compare, among other things, the concealment of the ultimatum to Belgium, the make-up of the German White Book, the elimination therefrom of the dispatch of the Czar on July 29,1914, etc. and it continues to maintain war sentiment among the people by the use of reprehensible methods."

Those letters show Liebknecht in his true light. He is not only, as some try to paint him, an opponent of this war, but is an opponent of all wars. He is not only committed to the fight against reaction at home, but to that against autocracy, wherever it exists.

On June 28, 1916, Karl Liebknecht was sentenced to thirty months' penal servitude. The trial was secret. When the public prosecutor asked for this secrecy Liebknecht exclaimed: "It is cowardice on your part, gentlemen. yes, I repeat, that you are cowards if you close these doors. You should be ashamed of yourself." Despite this protest the public was excluded.

When the news of the sentence was conveyed to the people crowding outside of the court room, a cry went forth, "Our Liebknecht has been condemned to two years and a half imprisonment. Long live Liebknecht!"

An appeal was made, but resulted only in an increase in the term of sentence to one of more than four years, and further appeal was denied. At present, Liebknecht is in prison making shoes, presumably, some one asserted, to help the Prussian government to stand on its feet. Sentenced, as he is to penal servitude, it is impossible for him to practice law again, and his legal career seems thus a thing of the past. The German ruling class has now accomplished. its object. It has Karl Liebknecht, one of the noblest and truest fighters for democracy and freedom, safely behind prison bars.

In all his agitation against war and militarism, and against political despotism, Karl Liebknecht has proved a worthy son of a great sire. Whenever he enters a fight which he deems a righteous one, he throws into it his whole being, regardless of personal consequences. His unfailing courtesy and hospitality are recognized by all who know him. "To meet him is to love him," is a phrase not inappropriately bestowed when applied to this fighter for democracy.

A brief sketch of Liebknecht may be of interest. He was born in Leipzig in August, 1871, the same year that his father was arrested on the charge of high treason. He studied first in Leipzig and then in Berlin, where he attended the University. From this institution he received his doctor's degree in political economy and law.

Liebknecht began his career of social enlightenment by organizing literary societies for the study of social problems. Later in Berlin he became active in the Socialist movement. His law office he had three partners, of whom two were his brothers was always a mecca for the oppressed. Almost any day, waiting in that office for Liebknecht who would reach there after his duties were over at the Reichstag, the Landtag or the Common Council, one would find audiences of many kinds. Some would be there to consult him on legal matters; some were students from home and abroad desiring personal advice and material help. Here was one looking for a position; another, desiring Liebknecht's help in getting articles published in the Socialist press; a third seeking information about entrance conditions at the university; still another anxious to be spared from police persecution. All were received with the utmost courtesy. All obtained a word of advice and help from "our Karl," as his friends call him.

In private life, Liebknecht has proved a fond husband and a loving father. His present wife his first is deceased is a Russian by birth, a graduate of the University of Heidelberg, and is an ideal life companion.

Liebknecht's vision has often proved prophetic. I remember well the conversation I had with him in 1912, just after the outbreak of the first Balkan, war when all Europe was on the qui vive, expecting momentarily that the Balkan war would spread throughout the continent. I arrived in Berlin rather late in the evening, immediately went to Liebknecht's office, and while traveling home with him discussed the political situation. Bethmann-Hollweg had delivered a speech in the Reichstag that very day.

"This speech," remarked Liebknecht, in a tone filled with seriousness, "has made it clear to me that Germany will back up Austria under all circumstances."

"How long would it take Germany to mobilize?" I asked him.

"About thirty-six hours," he declared. And from Liebknecht's tone one could see that he had the picture of the world tragedy before his eyes. I asked him what position the Socialists would take. He paused long and finally answered the question with a grave "It depends." There was something in the man's face and tone that haunted me, that now makes me certain that Liebknecht then had a very clear vision of the dark days ahead for the socialist movement and for the world.

What the future holds in store for Liebknecht, no one can tell. It may be predicted with some degree of assurance, however, that his activities are by no means over. The world, with justice, expects much from him in the days that are to come.

The foregoing constitutes but a brief and inadequate sketch of the activities of Liebknecht by a personal friend who believes that in him the world will recognize one of the most heroic figures of the present crisis and that the day is near when all Germany will proclaim him the man above all others who "sowed the seed that freedom men might reap," and that not only in Germany.

A PERSONAL FRIEND OF KARL LIEBKNECHT

# I.
## THE NATURE AND SIGNIFICANCE OF MILITARISM.

Militarism! There are few catch-words which are so frequently used to-day. There is scarcely another one which signifies something so complex, many-sided, Protean, or expresses a phenomenon so interesting and significant in its origin and nature, its means and effects a phenomenon so deeply rooted in the very nature of societies divided in classes, and which yet can adopt such extraordinarily multifarious shapes in societies of equal structure, all according to the physical, political, social, and economic conditions of states and territories.

Militarism is one of the most important and energetic manifestations of the life of most social orders, because it exhibits in the strongest, most concentrated, exclusive manner the national, cultural, and class instinct of self-preservation, that most powerful of all instincts.

A history of militarism, carried out with fundamental thoroughness, would comprise the very essence of the history of human development, lay bare its main-springs; and an investigation of capitalistic militarism would bring to light the most deeply hidden and delicate root-fibres of capitalism. Again, the history of militarism would be the history of the strained relations and jealousies between nations and states, arising from their desires for political and social power or economic advantage; at the same time it would be the history of class-struggles within nations and states for the same objects.

This is not even an attempt to write such a history; only some universal historical facts will be pointed out.

### ORIGIN AND FOUNDATION OF FORMS OF SOCIAL DOMINATION.

In the last analysis the superiority of *physical force* is the decisive factor in social domination. In its social aspect such physical force does not appear as the greater bodily strength of some individuals, it rather presupposes the equality of bodily strength of men, taken in the average, superiority thus resting purely: with the majority. Such a numerical relation does not necessarily correspond with the numerical relationship existing between groups of people having interests opposed to each other. Inasmuch as not everybody knows his own real interests, especially not his fundamental interests, and inasmuch as not everybody knows and recognizes the interests of his class as his own individual interests, it is materially determined by the extensive and intensive development of class-consciousness, which in its turn depends upon the mental and moral stage of evolution reached by a class. Again, that mental and moral stage of evolution is determined by the economic position of the various groups of interests (classes), whilst the social and political condition presents itself rather as a consequence as a consequence, it is true, which also has strong reactions as an expression of social domination.

The purely economic superiority also helps to cause *directly* a shifting and confusing of that numerical relation, inasmuch as economic pressure not only influences the mental and moral stage of development and therefore the ability to recognize class-interest, but also produces a tendency to act in opposition to a class-interest which is more or less recognized. That also the political machinery provides that class in whose hands it is with further means of domination with which to "correct" that numerical relationship in favor of the ruling group of interests is shown by four institutions well known to all police, law courts, schools, and church, which latter must also be reckoned among these institutions which the political machinery creates in its legislative function in order to exploit them for the application of the law and administrative purposes. The first two act chiefly by means of threats, deterrents and force, the school makes it its business to stop as effectively as possible the channels through which class-consciousness might find a way to hearts and brains, the church has a most effective way in providing men with blinkers, arousing their desires for a make-believe heavenly bliss and exploiting their fear of an infernal chamber of torture.

But not even the numerical relation thus altered can be considered as deciding the form of social domination. An armed man multiplies his physical power by means of his weapon. The extent of such multiplication depends upon the development of armament, including fortification and strategy, the forms of which result mainly from the development of armaments. The intellectual and economic superiority of one group of interests to another transforms itself directly, in consequence of the armament or better armament of the superior class, into a physical superiority and thus creates the possibility of a class-conscious majority being completely dominated by a class-conscious minority.

Though class-division is determined by economic conditions the relative political power of the classes is only in the first line determined by the economic condition of the various classes, in the second line by numerous intellectual, moral and physical means of exercising power, which in their turn pass into the hands of the ruling economic class by reason of its economic position. All these methods of exercising power can not influence the continued existence of classes, as that existence is safeguarded by a situation which is independent of them and which by necessity forces and maintains certain classes (even if these form a majority) in economic dependence on other classes, which may be a small minority, without the class-struggle or any means of political power being able to change it.(1)

The class-struggle can thus only be a struggle to develop class-consciousness, including a readiness for revolutionary action and sacrifice in the interest of the class, among its members, and a struggle for obtaining those means of power which are important for creating or suppressing class-consciousness, as well as those bodily and intellectual means of power the possession of which signifies a multiplication of physical force.

All this makes it clear what an important rôle the development of armament plays in social struggles. It decides whether it is not, or no longer, an economic necessity that a minority should continue, at least for a time, to rule over a majority against the will of the latter by military action, that "most concentrated political action." Apart from class-division the evolution of the forms of domination is actually everywhere closely bound up with the development of armament. As long as virtually everybody, even those in the most disadvantageous economic position, can procure arms of essentially equal value under practically the same difficulties, democracy, the reign of the majority principle, will as a rule be the political form of the society. That ought to be true even in societies divided in economic classes if only that one condition mattered. But in the natural course of development class-division, the result of economic evolution, runs parallel with the development of arms (including fortification and strategy), the manufacture of arms becoming thereby more and more a special skilful profession, and, as class rule corresponds as a rule with the economic superiority of one class, and the improvement in the manufacture of armament makes it continually more difficult and expensive to produce arms,(2) the manufacture of arms becomes gradually a monopoly of the ruling economic class, whereby that physical basis of democracy is done away with. And then we begin to hear the word: Possess and you are in the right. Even when a class possessing the political means of power loses its economic ascendancy it can at least for a time maintain its political rule.

It need scarcely be explained here that it is thus not only the form and nature of political domination which is partly conditioned by the development of armament, but also the form and nature of the prevailing class-struggles.

However, it is not sufficient that all citizens are equally armed and carry their arms in order to safeguard the continued existence of the rule of democracy, for the equal distribution of arms does not exclude the possibility, as the events in Switzerland have proved, that such distribution is abolished by a majority which is becoming a. minority, or even by a minority which is organized in a better, more efficient manner. The equal arming of the whole population can only endure and not be done away with when the *production of arms* can be carried on universally.

In his curious utopia, "The Coming Race," Bulwer described in an ingenious way the democratizing part which the development 'of armament can play. He imagines a stage of scientific development at which every citizen, provided with an easily procurable little staff charged with a mysterious force similar to electricity, is able at any moment to produce the most destructive effects. Indeed, we may expect science, the easy mastering of the most tremendous natural forces by man, to reach such a stage, however distant that time may be, at which the application of the science of murder on the battlefield will become an impossibility because it would mean the self-destruction of the human race, and at which the exploitation of scientific progress is transformed again as it were from a plutocratic into a democratic, universally human possibility.

### SOME FACTS FROM THE HISTORY OF MILITARISM.

In the lowest civilizations where class-division is unknown, arms, as a rule, serve as implements of labor. They serve for the acquisition of food (for the chase, for digging roots), also as a protection against wild animals, as a defence against hostile tribes and for attacking the latter. They are of such primitive nature that everybody can procure them easily at any time (stones and sticks, spears with flint heads, bows, etc.). The same is true of the *means of defence.* As there is not yet any division of labor worth mentioning, except for the most primitive of all divisions of labor, that between man and woman, all members of the community performing approximately the same social function exercised by their respective sexes, thus, as there do not yet exist any economic or political forms of domination armament cannot be the prop of such forms of domination within the community. Even if forms of domination existed arms could not support them. With armament in its primitive stage of development only democratic forms of rule are possible.

In those lowest civilizations arms can at most be used within the community for settling individual conflicts, but a change takes place as soon as class-division and the art of manufacturing arms develop. The original communism of the lower agricultural peoples with their gynarchy (rule of women) knows no social, and therefore as a rule, also no political domination of classes. In general, militarism can not develop; external complications, it is true, force such peoples to be prepared for war and produce temporarily even military despotism, a very frequent phenomenon with pastoral peoples on account of the warlike situations they encounter and because they regularly divide in classes at an earlier time.

We next remind the reader of the constitution of the Greek and Roman armies in which they find, according to class-division, a purely military hierarchy, organized on the basis of class, the armament of each file depending upon the class to which the soldier belonged. Let the reader also remember the armies of the feudal knights, with their following of much worse armed and protected squires who, according to Patrice Laroque, played rather the part of assistants to the combatants than that of combatants. The reason why the rulers in those times allowed and even brought about the arming of the lower orders is to be sought much less in the small degree of general security which the state could offer to the interests of the individual which it recognized (a want of security which thus made the arming of all necessary in a certain sense), than in the necessity of arming the nation or state for attack and defence against the foreign foe as well as was possible. The difference in the armament of the various classes of society assured at all times the possibility of employing the science of arms for the maintenance or the establishment of rule. The Roman slave wars exhibit this side of the question in a remarkable light.

The subject is also strongly illuminated by the German Peasants' War and the wars of the German cities. Among the chief direct causes of the unhappy outcome of the German Peasants' War must be reckoned the better military equipment of the clerico-feudal armies. However, the wars carried on by the cities in the XIVth century against those very armies were successful, not only because the art of making fire-arms was in an extraordinarily undeveloped stage as compared with the time of the Peasants' War of 1525, but above all because of the great economic power of the cities.

As locally organized social spheres of interest, they concentrated the members of those spheres, without any appreciable admixture of elements with different interests, in a narrow space; again, on account of their construction the cities occupied at the outset a tactical position of about the same importance as the feudal lords possessed, as Church and Emperor had in their castles and fortresses (this is likewise an element of military art — fortification); and, finally, the cities were themselves the chief producers of arms. Their citizens were indeed the superior representatives of the technical arts which annihilated the army of the knights.(3)

Particular attention must be paid to a result of the study of the Peasants' War and the wars of the cities, namely, to the importance of the various social classes living either in local separation or locally mixed. Where class-division corresponds with local division the class-struggle is facilitated, not only because class-consciousness is promoted thereby, but also because, from a purely technical point of view, the military concentration of the members of a class, as well as the production and the supply of arms are made easier. That happy local grouping of classes has favored all bourgeois revolutions; (4) it is almost lacking in the case of the proletarian revolution.(5)

The armies of mercenaries, which existed up to our own time, exhibit, like the question of armament, the direct transformation of economic power into physical power according to the Mephistophelian prescription:

> "If I can purchase stallions six
> Are not their powers mine a-plenty?
> I journey on and am a mighty man
> As if I had legs four and twenty."

Together with the further maxim, *divide et impera*, it is also being followed in establishing the so-called *élite* of an army. On the other hand, the example of the Italian condottieri, like that of the prætorian guards of earlier times, plainly demonstrates how much political power can be wielded through the possession of arms, military practice and the art of strategy. The mercenary boldly seized the crowns of princes, tossed them hither and thither, and became the natural candidate for the highest power in the; state,(6) a phenomenon repeatedly witnessed in times of excitement and war when military power is readily manipulated by individuals, even in our own age, e. g., Napoleon and his generals, also — Boulanger!

The history of the German "Wars of Liberation" furnishes important information about the influence of the external political situation on the development of armies and militarism. When, after the pitiful failure of the wars of the Coalition against the French Revolution, the feudal a armies of Frederick the Great had been crushed as in a mortar by the citizen army of France in 1806, the helpless German governments confronted the alternative either to surrender unconditionally to the Corsican conqueror or to vanquish him with his own weapon, with a citizen army, constituted by the general arming of the people. Their instinct of self-preservation and the spontaneous impulse of the people forced them to choose the second path. Then began that great period of the democratization of Germany, especially Prussia, brought about by external pressure, a period in which the political, social and economic strains in the interior were temporarily alleviated. Money and enthusiastic fighters for liberty were wanted. The human being increased in value. His social function as a creator of values and presumptive payer of taxes and his natural physical quality as the embodiment of strength, intelligence and enthusiasm gained a decisive importance, and caused his value to rise, as is ever the case in times of general peril, whilst the influence of class-differentiation diminished. The Prussian people had "learned to suppress all strife under the long endured foreign yoke," to use the jargon of the military weekly gazette. As has so often been the case, the financial and military questions played a revolutionary part. Many economic, social and political obstacles were removed. Industry and commerce, financially of chief importance, were promoted as far as it was possible with the peddling democratic spirit of Prussia-Germany. Even political liberties were introduced or at least promised. The people rose in arms, the storm burst forth, the army of Scharnhorst and Gneisenau, the army of the general arming of the people chased the "hereditary enemy" across the Rhine in the great Wars of Liberation, and prepared a miserable end for the world conqueror who had undermined the France of the Great Revolution, though that army was not even the democratic institution Scharnhorst and Gneisenau had wanted to create. The German people, like the Moor in "Fiesco," having done their duty, duly received the "thanks of the House of the Habsburgs." The Carlsbad resolutions (7) followed the Battle of the Nations at Leipzig, and after the pressure from without had been removed and all the demons of reaction had been let loose again on the people, one of the most important measures of the Metternich (8) system of perjured and accursed memory, was the destruction of the democratic army of the Wars of Liberation. The highly civilized regions of Germany might have been ripe for that army, but it collapsed abruptly, together with nearly all the fine things the great popular rising had brought, under the leaden weight of the junker barbarism, having its seat east of the Elbe.

A superficial glance at the development of armies shows the strong dependence of the constitution and size of an army not merely on social organization, but also, and in far greater measure, on the development of armament. The revolutionizing effect which, for instance, the invention of fire-arms had in that direction is one of the most conspicuous facts in the history of war.

## II.
## CAPITALISTIC MILITARISM.

### PRELIMINARY REMARKS.

Militarism is not specifically a capitalistic institution. It is, on the contrary, an institution peculiar and essential to all societies divided in classes, of which capitalist society is the last. It is true that capitalism develops, like every other society divided in classes, a kind of militarism peculiar to itself,(9) for militarism is in its nature a means to an end, or to several ends, which differ with the kind of the society and which are to be attained in various ways according to the different characters of the societies. That fact appears not only in the constitution of the army, but also in the remaining substance of militarism which mani tests itself in the tasks militarism has to accomplish.

Best adapted to the capitalistic stage of development is the army built on universal military science which, though an army constituted by the people, is not an army of the people, but an army against the people, or becomes increasingly. converted into such a one.

Now it appears in the shape of a standing army, now as a militia. The standing army,(10) which is likewise not an institution peculiar to capitalism, appears as its most developed, and even its normal form, this will be shown in the following pages.

### "MILITARISM FOR ABROAD," NAVALISM AND COLONIAL MILITARISM. POSSIBILITIES OF WAR AND DISARMAMENT.

The army of the capitalist order of society serves a double purpose, like the army of the other social systems.

It is, in the first place, a national institution destined for attack abroad or for the protection against a danger coming from abroad, in short, designed for international complications or, to use a military catch-phrase, against the foreign enemy.

That function has in no way been done away with by more recent developments. For capitalism war is indeed, in Moltke's phrase, "a part of God's world order."(11) It is true that there exists in Europe itself at least a tendency to eliminate certain causes of war, and the probability of a war originating in Europe itself decreases more and more, in spite of Alsace-Lorraine, the anxiety about the trio, Clemenceau, Pichon, Picquart, in spite of the Eastern Question, in spite of pan-islamism, and in spite of the revolution going on in Russia. In their place, however, new and highly dangerous causes of friction have arisen in consequence of the desires for commercial and political expansion (12) cherished by the so-called "civilized nations," desires which are mainly responsible for the Eastern Question and pan-islamism, and in consequence of world politics, especially colonial politics which, as Chancellor Bulow frankly recognized in the Reichstag, on November 14, 1906,(13) contains innumerable possibilities. (14) Of conflict and forces to the front ever more vigorously two other forms of militarism — *navalism* and *colonial militarism*. We Germans can tell a story of that!

*Navalism,* militarism on sea, is the natural brother of land militarism and shows all its repulsive and vicious traits. It is in a still greater degree than land militarism is at present not only an effect, but also a cause of international dangers, of the danger of a world war.

Some good folk and deceivers want to make us believe that the strained relations between Germany and England (15) are merely the result of some misunderstandings, agitations of mischievous journalists, the braggings of unskilful diplomatists; but we know better. We know that these strained relations are a necessary result of the increasing economic competition between Germany and England in the world's markets, a direct result of the unbridled capitalistic development and international competition. The Spanish-American War for Cuba, Italy's Abyssinian War, England's South African War, the Chinese-Japanese War, the Chinese adventure of the Great Powers, the Russian-Japanese War, all of them, however different their special causes and the conditions from which they sprung might have been, yet exhibit the one great common characteristic feature of wars of expansion. And if we remember the strained relations between England and Russia on account of Thibet, Persia and Afghanistan, the disagreements between Japan and the United States in the winter of 1906, and finally the Morocco conflict of glorious memory with the Franco-Spanish coöperation of December, 1906, (16) we must recognize that the capitalistic policy of colonization and expansion has placed numerous mines under the edifice of world peace, mines whose fuses are in many hands and which can explode very easily and unexpectedly.(17) It is certainly thinkable that a time may come when the division of the world has progressed to such an extent that a policy of placing all possible colonial possessions in trust for the colonial empires becomes feasible, thus eliminating colonial competition, as has been accomplished in regard to private capitalist competition to a certain extent by the combines and trusts. But that is a distant possibility which the economic and national rise of China alone may defer for an incalculable space of time.

All the alleged *plans for disarmament* are thus seen to be for the present nothing but foolery, phrase-making and attempts at deception. The fact that the Czar was the chief originator of the comedy at the Hague puts the true stamp on all of them.

Indeed, in our own days-the bubble of an alleged English disarmament burst in a ridiculous fashion. Secretary for War Hilton, the alleged promoter of those intentions, came out in strong words as an opponent of each and every reduction of the active military forces and showed himself as a true military hotspur, (18) whilst at the same time the Anglo-French military convention appeared above the horizon. Moreover, at the very hour when preparations were being made for the second "Peace Conference," Sweden increased her fleet, America (19) and Japan saw their military budgets mount higher and higher, and the Clémenceau government in France demanded an increase of 208 millions, (20) dwelt upon the necessity of a strong army and navy, the *Hamburger Nachrichten* [an important semi-official German newspaper] was describing the unshakeable faith in the holy savior Militarism as the quintessence of the feeling dominating Germany's ruling classes, and the German people were treated by their government to increased military demands (21) which were greedily grasped at even by our Liberals.(22) Such facts give us a measure of the naïveté displayed by the French Senator, d'Estournelles de Constant, a member of the Hague Tribunal, in an essay on the limitation of armaments.(23) Indeed, in the imagination of this political dreamer it needs not even the proverbial swallow to make the summer of disarmament, a simple sparrow will do. After that it is almost refreshing to encounter the honest brutality with which the great powers at the conference dropped Mr. Stead's proposals and refused even to place the question of disarmament on the agenda of the second conference.

A few more remarks must be made about the third offspring of capitalism on the military side, viz., *colonial militarism*. The colonial army (by this is meant not the colonial militia, (24) as planned for German Southwest Africa, still less the entirely different militia of the almost independent British colonies) is of extraordinarily great importance for England, and its importance is also increasing for the other civilized countries. Whilst for England it not only fulfils the task of oppressing and keeping in check the colonial "interior enemy," i.e., the natives of the colonies, but also constitutes a weapon against the exterior colonial enemy, Russia, for instance, it serves the other colonizing powers, especially America and Germany, often under the names of "Schutztruppe" (protective troops) or foreign legion, (25) almost exclusively for the first named purpose, that of driving the miserable natives to slave in the bagnios for capitalism, and to shoot and cut them down and starve them without pity whenever they attempt to protect their country against the foreign conquerors and extortioners. The colonial army, which frequently consists of the scum of the European population, (26) is the most brutal and abominable of all the tools employed by our capitalistic states. There is hardly a crime which colonial militarism and savage tropical brutality [*Tropenkoller,* the Germans call it], directly cultivated by it, have not produced. (27) The names of Tippelskirch, Woermann, Podbielski, Leist, Wehlau, Peters, Ahrenberg, and others testify and prove it for Germany, too. They are the fruit by which the nature of the policy of colonization can be known, that colonial policy which, pretending (28) to spread Christianity of civilization or to protect national honor, piously practices usury and fraud for the advantage of capitalists interested in colonies, which murders and-violates defenceless human beings, burns down the possessions of the defenceless, robbing and pillaging them, mocking and disgracing Christianity and civilization.(29) Even the fame of a Cortez or a Pizarro fades before India and Tongking, the Congo, German Southwest Africa and the Philippines.

## THE PROLETARIAT AND THE WAR

It the function of militarism was above defined as being a national one directed against the foreign enemy it must not be understood to mean that it is a function answering the interests, welfare and wishes of the capitalistically governed and exploited peoples. The proletariat of the whole world can not expect any profit from the policies which make necessary the "militarism for abroad", its interests are most sharply opposed to such policies. Directly or indirectly those policies serve the exploiting interests of the ruling classes of capitalism. They are policies which prepare more or less skilfully, the way for the world-wide expansion of the wildly anarchical mode of production and the senseless and murderous competition of capitalism, in which process all the duties of civilized man towards the less developed peoples are flung aside; and yet nothing is really attained except an insane imperiling of the whole existence of our civilization in consequence of the warlike world complications that are conjured up. The working-class, too, welcome the immense economic developments of our days. But they also know that this economic development could be carried on peacefully without the mailed fist, without militarism and navalism, without the trident being in our hand and with out the barbarities of our colonial system, if only sensibly managed communities were to carry it on according to international understandings and in conformity with the duties and interests of civilization. They knew that our world policy largely explains itself as an attempt to fight down and confuse forcibly and clumsily the social and political home problems confronting the ruling classes, in short, as an attempt at a policy of deceptions and misreadings such as Napoleon III. was a master of. They know that the enemies of the working-class love to make their pots boil over the fires of narrow-minded jingoism, that the fear of war in 1887, unscrupulously engineered by Bismarck, did excellent service to the most dangerous forces of reaction, that according to a nice little plan, lately revealed, (30) and hatched by a number of highly placed personages, the Reichstag suffrage was to be filched from the German people in the excitement of jingoism, "after the return of a victorious army." They know that the advantages of the economic development which those policies attempt to exploit, especially all the advantages of our colonial policies, flow into the ample pockets of the exploiting class, of capitalism, the arch-enemy of the proletariat. They know that the wars the ruling classes engage in for their own purposes demand of the working-class the most terrible sacrifice of blood and treasure,(31) for which they are recompensed, after the work has been done, by miserable pensions, beggarly grants to war invalids, street organs and kicks.

They know that after every war a veritable mud-volcano of Hunnic brutality and baseness sends its floods over the nations participating in it, rebarbarizing all civilization for years.(32) The worker knows that the fatherland for which he is to fight is not his fatherland; that there is only one real enemy for the proletariat of every country the capitalist class who oppresses and exploits the proletariat, that the proletariat of every country is by its most vital interests closely bound to the proletariat of every other country, that all national interests recede before the common interests of the international proletariat, and that the international coalition of exploiters and oppressors must be opposed by the international coalition of the exploited and oppressed. He knows that the proletarians, if they were to be employed in a war, would be led to fight against their own brethren and the members of their own class, and thus against their own interests. The class-conscious proletarian therefore not only frowns upon that international purpose of the army and the entire capitalist policy of expansion, he is fighting them earnestly and with understanding. To the proletariat falls the chief task of fighting militarism in that direction, too, to the utmost, and it is more and more becoming conscious of that task, which is shown by the international congresses; by the exchange of protestations of solidarity between the German and French Socialists at the outbreak of the Franco-German War of 1870, between the Spanish and American Socialists at the outbreak of the war about Cuba, between the Russian and Japanese Socialists at the outbreak of the war in eastern Asia in 1904, and by the resolution to declare a general strike in case of war between Sweden and Norway, adopted by the Swedish Social Democrats. It was further shown by the parliamentary attitude of the German Social Democracy towards the war credits of 1870 and during the Morocco conflict, as also by the attitude taken up by the class-conscious proletariat towards intervention in Russia.

## FUNDAMENTAL FEATURES OF "MILITARISM FOR HOME" AND ITS PURPOSE

Militarism does not only serve for defence and attack against the foreign enemy; it has a second task, (33) one which is being brought out ever more clearly with the growing accentuation of class antagonism, defining ever more clearly the form and nature of militarism, viz., that of protecting the existing state of society, that of being a pillar of capitalism and all reactionary forces in the war of liberation engaged in by the working-class. Here it shows itself purely as a weapon in the class struggle, a weapon in the hands of the ruling classes, serving, in conjunction with the police and law-courts, school and church, the purpose of obstructing the development of class-consciousness and of securing, besides, at all costs to a minority the dominating position in the state and the liberty of exploiting their fellow-men, even against the enlightened will of the majority of the people.

This is modern militarism, which attempts nothing less than squaring the circle, which arms the people against the people itself, which, by trying with all means to force upon social division an artificial division according to ages, makes bold to turn the workman into an oppressor and an enemy, into a murderer of members of his own class and his friends, of his parents, sisters and brothers and children, into a murderer of his own past and future; which pretends to be democratic and despotic, enlightened and mechanical, popular and anti-popular at the same time.

It must, however, not be forgotten that militarism can also turn the point of its sword against the interior national, and even the interior (34) religious "enemy" (in Germany, for instance, against the Poles, (35) Alsatians and Danes), and can moreover be employed in conflicts among the non-proletarian classes, that militarism is a highly polymorphous phenomenon, capable of many changes, and that the Prusso-German militarism has attained a peculiarly flourishing state in consequence of the peculiar semi-absolutist, feudal bureaucratic conditions of Germany. This Prusso-German militarism is endowed with all the bad and dangerous qualities of any form of capitalist militarism, so that it is best suited to serve as a paradigm for showing militarism in its present stage, in its forms, means and effects. As nobody has as yet succeeded, to use a Bismarckian phrase, in imitating our Prussian lieutenants, nobody has as yet been fully able to imitate our Prusso-German militarism, which has not only become a state within the state, but positively a state above the state.

Let us first consider the army systems of some other countries. In doing so we must take into consideration not only the army proper, but also the constabulary and police forces, which frequently appear to be merely special military organizations for everyday use against the interior enemy, but betray their military origin by their very violence and brutality.

## ARMY SYSTEMS OF SOME FOREIGN COUNTRIES

We encounter peculiar forms in the army systems of countries such as England and America, Switzerland and Belgium.

*Great Britain*(36) has a mercenary army ("regular army"), a militia with a mounted yeomanry; besides, the so-called Volunteers, a force voluntarily recruited which, on the whole, is unpaid and numbered 245,000 men in 1905. The standing army, including the militia (in which the furnishing of substitutes is permitted) numbered 444,000 men in 1905, of whom however only some 162,000 were stationed in England. For Ireland there exists, moreover, a militarily organized police force of some 12,000 men. The standing army is largely employed abroad, especially in India, where two-thirds of the army of almost 230,000 (37) men consists of natives. The colonies have, as a rule, their own militias and volunteer forces. The relation between Great Britain's home and colonial militarism is characterized by the military budget, which, in 1897, was about 360 million marks for the home country and about 510 million marks for India. To this must be added the immense fleet, with crews and marines numbering almost 200,000 men.

The army system of the United States is a mixture of standing army and militia. The army, which is made up by recruiting (38) and is by law limited to a maximum strength of 100,000 men, numbers in times of peace, according to the enlisted strength of 1905, 61,000 men (on October 15, 1906, including the Philippine Scouts, 67,253 men), among them 3,800 officers, mostly educated at the military academy at West Point. In the same year the militia numbered some 111,000 men. The militia is organized on a fairly democratic basis. In times of peace it is under the control of the governors of the various states, and its armament and training is not in accordance with modern efficiency. Besides, an important part is played by the police force, frequently organized on a military basis.

Of quite an original kind is another institution which, considered in its formal aspect, does not fall within the frame of this chapter, but which, however, must not be left unmentioned in this connection on account of the function it performs. In all the capitalist countries we find the gun-men of the employers, even if, in some cases, they be only strike-breakers armed by the employers. (This is no rare occurrence in Switzerland and France, for instance, and as to Germany we refer the reader to the Hamburg ship-builders' strike and the incidents at Nuremberg in 1906). But the American capitalists have at all times at their disposal such a band of gun-men of prime quality in the shape of the armed Pinkerton detectives. Finally, taking into consideration some 30,000 men in the American navy, in 1905, we see that the United States, too, furnishes a choice collection of the main forms of the armed forces of the state.

In *Switzerland* there existed until lately a real people's army, a general arming of the people. Every Swiss citizen, able to bear arms, had his gun and ammunition continually in his house. That was the army of democracy of which Gaston Moch treats in his well-known book. Switzerland enjoying an international guarantee equal to that of Belgium, it was only natural that in this country "militarism for abroad" should assume and retain a particularly mild character, a result to which numerous other circumstances contributed their share. But the "militarism for home" changed with the accentuation of class antagonism. The fact that the proletariat possessed arms and ammunition was increasingly felt, by the capitalist class that wanted to dominate, to be an impediment to its liberty to exploit and oppress and even a danger to its existence. So, in September, 1899, they began to disarm the people by taking its cartridges away and endeavoring at the same time to develop with continually increasing vigor the existing rudiments of militarism in the direction of the institutions of the great military powers. Attempts were made to transform successively the active portions of the army into a willing instrument of class domination by all the means employed by those military powers. In that way the celebrated Swiss militia developed more and more the repellent traits which have made all standing armies a disgrace to civilization. Nothing has been changed by the resolution on the employment of soldiers in strikes which was passed by the National Council, on December 21, 1906, in connection with the law on military organization.

Because of her neutrality, *Belgium's* demand for soldiers for her standing army is considerably smaller (by about one-half) than her "stock" of material for soldiering. On that account the system of universal military service is modified by a *draft system* (drawing lots) and by the *substitute* system, which latter deeply influences the character of the army. Naturally, only the well-to-do are able to furnish substitutes, and they as naturally make the widest use of it. At first that system of furnishing substitutes, which was formerly so general, may not have been of any special political significance, but in Belgium it has led to a result very serious for the ruling class, as the country possesses a numerous proletariat and the percentage of workmen is very great among the men liable to military service and drawn by lot. Even that portion of the proletarian Belgian army which did not consist of class-conscious proletarians and proletarians ready to risk all, so rapidly succumbed to the anti-militarist propaganda that for years past it has not had any value as a weapon in the hands of the ruling class against the interior enemy and is no longer used as such. But they found a way out of the difficulty. From former times there existed an institution, called the civic guard. To the civic guard belong those who have drawn a lucky number and have furnished substitutes, but only if they can buy their own uniforms and arms, a condition almost excluding the poorer population. It used to be nothing but a fancy-dress parade, its members were mostly Liberals, its organization, democratic. Members of the civic guard kept their arms at home, elected their own officers, etc. A change was brought about in consequence of the increasing untrustworthiness of the standing army. The administration and management of the civic guard were taken out of the hands of the municipalities and transferred to those of the government, the democratic institutions were abolished, and the arms were taken away from the individuals and locked away in the depots of the military administration. A fairly rigorous system of military drill was introduced, and the training of the civic guard was confided to the most objectionable characters among the former officers of the standing army. Men between the ages of 20 and 30 have to train no less than three nights a week and on half of a Sunday every two weeks, and if formerly those military exercises reminded one of the happy-go lucky functions of our German civic soldiers of olden days, they are now carried out under a sharp control and punctuality is enforced by punishments. It is to be noted that this reorganization of the civic guard has only taken place in communities of more than 20,000 inhabitants, whilst in the other places the civic guard has remained a ridiculous presence. That fact, too, marks the civic guard to be a special force of the government in the struggle against the "interior enemy." Excluding the military police, the standing army numbered, in 1905, about 46,000 men; the active civic guard numbered about 44,000 men, almost as many.

Belgium thus possesses an army against the exterior, and a special army against the interior enemy, an exquisite arrangement which, as the employment of the civic guard during the late suffrage struggles and strikes has proved, renders and will continue to render good service to the capitalist regime in Belgium.

In addition, there is in Belgium the constabulary or military police, who have simply to perform military tasks in war as well as during strikes and riots. They are very numerous and spread all over the country, of great mobility, and can be concentrated, shifted and mobilized at a moment's notice, at Tervueren, near Brussels, they have general barracks for their flying brigade, and they swarm out during strikes and such like movements all over the country like a flight of wasps. Most of them are former non-commissioned officers of the army, they are well paid, excellently armed, in short, an elite force. Whilst the civic guard is as if created for its task in the class-struggle, because it represents nothing less than a special military mobilization of the capitalist bourgeoisie, which is well aware of its interests, the "watch-dogs" of capitalism, organized in the constabulary, play their part no less efficiently for the present, according to the rule that they must play the tune called for by him who pays the piper.

*Japan*, a country in about the same capitalist feudal stage of development as Germany, has in spite of her insular position, which is similar to that of England, and in consequence of her strained foreign relations, of late become even from a military point of view a veritable counterpart of Germany, except perhaps that her troops are given a more serviceable war training.

## CONCLUSIONS. RUSSIA

It follows from all this that the size and the particular character of the organization of an army accommodate themselves to the international situation, to the function the army has as regards the exterior enemy. The international tension is driving states (even those which are not yet capitalist and which compete with and have to protect themselves against the capitalist states) to train all citizens capable of bearing arms and to adopt the most rigorous form of military organization, the standing conscript army. This can be considerably relaxed by natural causes as, for instance, by the insular position of Great Britain or the comparatively insular situation of the United States, and by artificial political means as, for instance, the neutralization of Switzerland and the states of the Low Countries. But the function of "militarism for home," against the interior enemy, militarism as a weapon in the class-struggle, is an ever necessary accompanying feature of capitalist development, and even Gaston Moch regards the "re-establishment of order" as a "legitimate function of a people's army." The reason why "militarism for home" exhibits forms greatly differing from one another explains itself simply by the fact that such militarism has hitherto had a more national purpose, the fulfilment of which was not so much influenced by international competition, that therefore it can give much more consideration to national peculiarities. However, England and also America (a country in which the standing army was increased from 27,000 to about 61,000 men from 1896 to 1906, where the number of men in the war navy was doubled, the war budget multiplied by two and a half and the navy budget by three in the same space of time, and where Mr. Taft asked for 100 millions more for 1907), are being increasingly pushed into the paths of the militarism of the European continent. This is certainly caused in the first line by changes in the international situation and the requirements of jingo and imperialist world policy, but in the second line quite unmistakably by changes in the interior tension, the intensification of the class struggle. It is scarcely possible that the militaristic velleities of the British war secretary, Haldane, in September, 1906, have only a *temporal* relation to the energetic political activity of the British working-class. The propensity to introduce universal military training of the Swiss kind, which for the time being has been repulsed in England in spite of the strong agitation in favor of such training and which in the United States found significant expression in Mr. Roosevelt's message of December 4, 1906, is not a symptom of progress. It signifies, in spite of all said to the contrary, a strengthening of militarism as compared to its present condition, and is a station on the precipitous road leading to a standing army, as the example of Switzerland proves.

On account of the great multiplicity of possible combinations between the factors determining the extent and nature of the special requirements for protection against the exterior and interior enemy, militarism shows unmistakably a pronounced multiformity and transmutability. But that transmutability is always kept within the limits prescribed by the absolutely essential capitalistic purpose of militarism. Nevertheless, development may temporarily take directly opposite roads. While France, for example, under Picquart, is earnestly attacking the problem of greatly reducing the training period of her reserve and territorial troops, reforming the "biribiri" and abolishing separate military jurisdiction, the president of the German central military court, von Massow, quitted the service in the fall of 1906, because the military command (the Prussian war ministry) had on the strength of legal interpretation formally invaded the independence of the military courts, an independence which had indeed already received a curious construction by the disciplining of the judges acting in the Bilse case. French conditions are almost exclusively due to the prevailing anti-clericalism; clericalism has an important pillar in the army, the government needs the help of the proletariat for its anti-clerical policy. Such a combination is of course not of eternal duration, nor has it sprung from a real, lasting tendency of evolution. It results from a constellation, transient in its nature, and is quite compatible, as has been proved, with an energetic fight against anti militarism.

From these points of view an interesting case is furnished by Russia which has been forced to adopt universal military service on account of her intensely strained foreign relations, and which as an Asiatic despotic state is confronted by an interior discord without example. The interior enemy of Czarism is not only the proletariat, but also the immense mass of the peasantry and the bourgeoisie, and even a large portion of the nobility. Ninety-nine percent. of the Russian soldiers belong to classes that are the arch-enemies of the Czar's despotism. The development of class consciousness is extremely hampered by the low state of education, national and religious antagonisms and the clashes of economic and social interests; further by the greater or smaller pressure exercised by the widely ram)fied bureaucratic apparatus, by the unfavorable arrangement of political districts, the insufficiently developed means of communication, and other things. By a cunningly devised system of elite forces, like the constabulary and, above all, the Cossacks, who have been positively changed into a special social class by means of good pay and other material rewards, large political privileges and the establishment of semi-socialist Cossack communities, and are thus artificially bound to the despotic regime, Czarism attempts to secure a sufficiently strong band of faithful retainers to fight down the unrest which has penetrated deeply into the ranks of the army. In addition to these "watch-dogs of Czarism" there are the Circassians (40) and other barbarian populations living in the empire of the knout who, for instance, were let loose upon the land like a pack of wolves during the counterrevolution in the Baltic Province, and all the other armed beneficiaries of Czarism whose name is legion, the police and their accomplices, as well as the Russian toughs, the black bands. In the bourgeois capitalist state the conscript army, in its function as a weapon against the proletariat, is a crude and, at the same time, terrible and fantastic contradiction in itself, under the Czar's despotic regime the conscript army is a weapon which must 1:urn itself more and more with crushing power against the despotism of Czarism itself, from which at the same time the conclusion must be drawn that the experience derived from the antimilitarist developments in Russian *can be utilized only with great care in regard to the bourgeois capitalist states.* In the bourgeois capitalist states, the attempts of the ruling classes to buy the people to fight against itself, and that even largely with money taken from the people for the purpose mentioned, are condemned to ultimate failure. In regard to Russia, we are witnessing already how desperate and wretched attempts of Czarism to bribe the revolution, as it were, are resulting in an early and pitiable fiasco amidst the miseries of the financial situation, in spite of all the endeavors of the unscrupulous international stock-exchange financiers to retrieve the situation. It is certain that the loan question is an important one, at least in regard to the rate at which the revolution develops, but as little as revolutions can be artificially made as little and still less can they be bought, (41) even if the means of the high finance of the world should be employed.

## III
## MEANS AND EFFECTS OF MILITARISM.

### THE IMMEDIATE GOAL.

We now proceed to a special investigation of the means and effects of militarism, taking as a paradigm the Prusso-German bureaucratic, feudal and capitalist militarism, that worst form of capitalist militarism, that state above the state.

Though it is true that modern militarism is but an institution of our capitalist society, it is none the less true that it is an institution which has almost succeeded in becoming an independent institution; an end in itself.

In order to fulfil its purpose militarism must turn the army into a handy, docile, effective tool. It must raise its *equipment* to the highest possible perfection and, on the other hand, as the army is not composed of machines, but of men, being a kind of living machinery, it must inspire the army with the *proper* "spirit."

The *first* part of the problem is ultimately a question of finance, which will be dealt with later. We shall deal with the *second* part first.

The question presents *three* aspects. Militarism seeks to create and promote the military spirit above all and in the first line in the *active* army itself; secondly in those portions of the population furnishing the *reserves* of the army in case of mobilization; finally in all the *other parts of the population* that are of importance for militaristic and anti-militaristic purposes.

### MILITARY PEDAGOGY. TRAINING SOLDIERS.

That proper "military spirit," also called "patriotic spirit" and, in Prussia-Germany, "loyalty to the king," signifies in short a constant readiness to pitch into the exterior or the interior enemy whenever commanded to do so. Taken by itself the most suitable condition for its production is a state of complete stupidity, or at least as low an intelligence as possible which enables one to drive the mass as a herd of cattle in whatever direction is demanded by the interest of the "existing order." The avowal of the Prussian war minister, von Einem, who said that he liked a soldier loyal to his king, even he were a bad shot, better than a less loyal one however good a shot he might be, certainly came from the depth of the soul of this representative of German militarism. But here militarism finds itself in a bad quandary. The handling of arms, strategy and tactics demand of the modern soldier not a small measure of intelligence and cause the more intelligent soldier also to be the more efficient, *cæteris paribus*. For that reason alone militarism would no longer be able to do anything with a merely stupid mass of men. Moreover, capitalism could not use such a stupid mass, as the great mass of the people, especially the great mass of the proletariat, have to perform economic functions requiring intelligence. To be able to exploit, to secure the highest possible rate of profit — the task of its life which it cannot escape — capitalism is compelled by a tragical fate to foster systematically and to a large extent among its slaves the same intelligence which, as it knows quite well, must bring death and annihilation to capitalism. All the attempts to guide the ship of capitalism by skilful tacking, by a cunning cooperation of church and school, safely between the Scylla of too low an intelligence which would be too great an impediment to exploitation and would make the proletarian even unfit as a beast of burden, and the Charybdis of an education which revolutionizes the minds of the exploited, enabling them to grasp their class-interests in their entirety and necessarily bringing destruction to capitalism, must end in dreary and hopeless failure. It is only the East Elbian (42) farmhands (who still may be, as was once said, the most stupid workers indeed and the best workers — for the junkers, be it noted) who largely furnish militarism with human material that can be commanded in herds without trouble, purely like slaves, but can be used to advantage in the army only with care and within certain limits, on account of an intelligence which is even too low for militarism.

Our best soldiers are Social Democrats, is a much quoted expression. It shows the difficulty of the task of imbuing the conscript army with the proper military spirit. As the mere unquestioning and slavish (43) obedience does no longer suffice and is also no longer possible, militarism must seek to dominate the will of its human material by a roundabout way in order to create its shooting automata. It must bend the will by working upon the men's mind and soul or by force, it must decoy its pupils or coerce them. The proper 'spirit" needed by militarism for its purpose against the foreign enemy consists of a crazy jingoism, narrow-mindedness and arrogance, the spirit it needs for its purposes against the enemy at home is that of a lack of understanding or even hatred of every kind of progress, every enterprise and movement even distantly endangering the rule of the actually dominating class. It is in that direction that militarism, when moulding the character of its charges by its milder means, must turn the mind and sentiments of those soldiers whose class-interest removes them entirely from the sphere of jingoism and makes them see in every step in advance, including the overthrow of the existing order of society itself, the only reasonable goal to be aimed at. We do not deny that with the proletarian of military age class consciousness is usually not yet firmly rooted, though he generally greatly surpasses the bourgeois youth of the same age in independence of character and political understanding.

It is an extremely bold and cunning system, this system of moulding a soldier's intellect and feeling, which attempts to supplant the class division according to social status by a class-division according to ages, to create a special class of proletarians of the ages from 20 to 22, whose thinking and feeling are directly opposed to the thinking and feeling of the proletarians of a different age.

In the first place the proletarian in uniform must be separated locally, sharply and without any consideration, from members of his class and his own family. That purpose is attained by removing him from his home district, which has been accomplished systematically especially in Germany, and above all by shutting him up in barracks.(44) One might almost describe the system as a copy of the jesuitical method of education, a counter-part of the monastic institutions.

In the next place that segregation must be kept up as long a time as possible, a tendency which, as the military necessity of the long period of training has long since disappeared, is thwarted by untoward financial consequences. It was substantially that circumstance to which we owe the in troduction of the two-years' military service in 1892.

Finally, the time thus gained must be utilized as skilfully as possible to capture the souls of the young men. Various means are employed for that purpose.

All human weaknesses and senses must be appealed to to serve the system of military education, exactly as is done in the church. Ambition and vanity are stimulated, the soldier's coat is represented as the most distinguished of all coats, the soldier's honor is lauded as being of special excellence, and the soldier's status is trumpeted forth as the most important and distinguished and is indeed endowed with many privileges.(45) The love of finery is appealed to by turning the uniform, contrary to its purely military purpose, into a gay masquerade dress, to comply with the coarse tastes of those lower classes who are to be fascinated. All kinds of little glittering marks of distinction, marks of honor, cords for proficiency in shooting, etc., serve to satisfy the same low instinct, the love for finery and swagger. Many a soldier has had his woes soothed by the regimental band to which, next to the glittering gew-gaw of the uniforms and the pompous military ostentation, is due the greatest part of that unreserved popularity which our "magnificent war army" can amply boast of among children, fools, servant girls and the riff-raff. Whoever has but once seen the notorious public attending the parades and the crowds following the mounting of the Berlin palace guard must be clear on that point. It is sufficiently known that the popularity of the military uniform thus actually created among certain portions of the civilian population, is a factor of considerable importance to allure the uneducated elements of the army.

The lower the mentality of the soldiers, the lower their social condition, the better is the effect of all these means, for such elements are not only more easily deceived by tinsel and finery on account of their weak faculty of discernment, but to them the difference between the level of their former civilian existence and their military position also appears to be particularly great and striking. (One need only think of an American negro or an East Prussian agricultural slave suddenly invested with the "most distinguished coat.) There is thus a tragical conflict going on, in as much as those means have less effect with the intelligent industrial proletarian for whom they are intended in the first line, than with those elements that need hardly be influenced in that direction, for the present at least, since they furnish without them a sufficiently docile military raw material. However those means may in their case, too, contribute to the *preservation* of the "spirit" approved of by militarism. The same purpose is served by regimental festivals, the celebration of the Emperor's birthday, and other contrivances.

When everything has been done to get the soldier into the mood of drunkenness, as it were, to narcotize his soul, to inflame his feelings and imagination, his *reason* must be worked upon systematically. The daily military school lesson begins in which it is sought to drum into the soldier a childish, distorted view of the world, properly trimmed up for the purposes of militarism. This instruction, too, which is mostly given by entirely incapable and uneducated people, has no effect whatever on the more intelligent industrial proletarians, who are quite often much more intelligent than their instructors. It is an experiment on an unsuitable material, an arrow rebounding on him that shot it. That has only lately been proved, in a controversy with General Liebert about the anti-socialist instruction of soldiers, by *The Post* and Max Lorenz, with the acumen generated by the capitalist competition for profits.

To produce the necessary pliability and tractableness of *will* pipe-clay service, the discipline of the barracks, the canonization of the officer's (46) and non-commissioned officer's (47) coat, which in many respects appears to be truly sacrosanct and *legibas solutus,* have to do service, in short, discipline and control which bind the soldier as in fetters of steel in regard to all he does and thinks, on duty and off duty. Each and every one is ruthlessly bent, pulled and stretched in all directions in such a manner that the strongest back runs danger of being broken in bits and either bends or breaks.(48)

The zealous fostering of the "church" spirit, which was explicitly demanded as a special aim of military education in a resolution submitted to the budget commission of the Reichstag in the month of February, 1892, and then voted down (without prejudice, by the way), is another method of the kind to complete the work of military oppression and enslavement.

Military instruction and ecclesiastical influence are at one and the same time methods of kind persuasion and compulsion, but the latter mostly only in a carefully veiled fonn of application.

The most attractive bait that is employed to make up and fill the important standing formations of the army is the system of reengagement of men whose time has expired, who are given a chance to earn premiums as non-commissioned officers (49) and are promised employment in the civil service after they leave the army.(50) It is a most cunningly devised and dangerous institution which also infects our whole public life with the militaristic virus, as will be shown further on.

The whip of militarism, the method by which it forces men to obey, reveals itself above all in the disciplinary system,(51) in the military penal law with its ferocious threats for the slightest resistance against the so-called military spirit, in the military judiciary with its semi-mediaeval procedure, with its habit of meting out the most inhuman and barbaric punishments for the slightest insubordination and its mild treatment of the transgressions committed by superiors against their subordinates, with its habit of juggling away, almost on principle, the soldier's right of self-defence against his superiors. Nothing can arouse more bitter feeling against militarism and nothing can at the same time be more instructive than a simple perusal of the articles of war and the records of the military penal cases.

The disciplinary beatings (ragging) to which the officers of English grenadier guard regiments are wont to regale each other with a laudable democratic zeal deserve to be mentioned as a curiosity.

This chapter also includes the maltreatment of soldiers, which will be specially dealt with on a later occasion. It forms, it is true, not a legal, but in practice perhaps the most effective, of all violent disciplinary methods of militarism.

Thus they attempt to tame men as they tame animals. Thus the recruits are drugged, confused, flattered, bribed, oppressed, imprisoned, polished and beaten, thus one grain is added to the other and mixed and kneaded to furnish the mortar for the immense edifice of the army, thus one stone is laid upon the other in a well calculated fashion to form a bulwark against the forces of subversion.(52)

That all those methods of alluring, disciplining and coercing the soldier partake of the nature of a weapon in the class-struggle is made evident by the institution of the one-year volunteer. [Young men with high-school education, which in Germany can hardly be attained by youths belonging to the working class, have the privilege of serving but one year instead of two, paying for their food, lodgings, uniform, etc.] The bourgeois offspring, destined to become an officer of the reserves, is generally above the suspicion of harboring anti-capitalist, anti-militarist or subversive ideas of any description. Consequently he is not sent out of his home district, he need not live in the barracks, nor is he obliged to attend the military school- or the church, and he is even spared a large part of the pipe-clay drill. Of course, if he falls into the clutches of discipline and the military penal law, it is exceptional and usually with harmless results, and the habitual oppressors of the soldiers, though they frequently nourish a hatred against all "educated people," only rarely venture to lay hands on him. The education of officers furnishes a second striking proof for this thesis.

Of exceptional importance for the discipline of an army is *the coöperation of masses of men* which does away with the initiative of the individual to a large extent. In the army each individual is chained to all the rest like a galley slave, and is almost incapable of acting with freedom. The combined force of the hundreds of thousands forming the army prevents him with an overwhelming power from making the slightest movement of his own volition. All the parts of this tremendous organism, or rather of this tremendous machinery are not only subject to the suggestive influence of the word of command, but also to a separate hypnotism, a mass suggestion whose influence, however, would be *impotent* on an army composed of enlightened and resolute opponents of militarism.

The two tasks of militarism, as will be seen, do not at all harmonize always in the department of military education, but are often at cross-purposes. That is not only true of training, but also in regard to equipment. War training demands ever more imperatively a continuously growing measure of initiative on the part of the soldier. As a "watch-dog of capital" the soldier does not require any initiative, he is not even allowed to possess it, if his qualification as a suicide is not to be destroyed. In short, war against the foreign foe requires men; war against the foe at home, slaves, machines. And as regards equipment and clothes the gaudy uniforms, the glittering buttons and helmets, the flags, the parades, the cavalry charges and all the rest of the nonsense can not be dispensed with for producing the spirit necessary for the battle against the interior enemy, though in a war against the exterior enemy all these things would positively bring about a calamity; they are simply impossible.(53) That tragical conflict, the numerous aspects of which can not be dealt with exhaustively in this book, has not been comprehended by the well-intentioned critics of our militarism, who in their simplicity only use the standard applicable to a system of training for war.

That antagonism of interests within militarism itself, that self-contradiction from which it suffers, has the tendency of becoming more and more acute. Which of the two opposing sets of interest gets the upper hand depends at a given time on the relation existing between the tension in home and foreign politics. Here we see clearly a potential self-destruction of militarism.

When the war against the interior enemy, in case of an armed revolution, puts such great demands on military art that dressed-up slaves and machines no longer suffice to fight him down the last hour of the violent domination of the minority, of capitalistic oligarchy will also have struck. It is of sufficient importance for us to note that the described military spirit as such confuses and leads astray the proletarian class-consciousness and that militarism, by infecting our whole public life, serves capitalism with that spirit in all other directions, apart from the purely military, for instance, by creating and promoting proletarian docility in face of economic, social and political exploitation and by thwarting as much as possible the struggle for the liberation of the working class. We shall have to deal with this later on.

## SEMI-OFFICAL AND SEMI-MILITARY ORGANIZATION OF THE CIVIL POPULATION

Militarism also seeks to influence *those persons who do not yet or who no longer belong to the active army*, to as large an extent, for as long a period and as strongly as possible. It attempts to accomplish its purpose in the first place by arrogating to itself the greatest possible authority over those persons, for instance, by a system of control, by largely extending the military jurisdiction, the procedure by the military courts of honor (which is even employed against retired officers) and even the competence of the military command. This method is characterized with particular clearness in the muster of the reserve. soldiers, when the men called up are placed under military jurisdiction, which is claimed by the military authorities to last for the *whole day*, though it is manifestly against the law, there is not the slightest ground for establishing such a right, it is a simple usurpation. In this connection mention must further be made of the cadet corps and veterans, associations with their semi-official or semimilitary organization, their aping of the military get-up, fiddle-faddle and junketings. A chief part in that department of militaristic activity is played by the mischievous reserve-officer system, which carries the military caste spirit into the civilian society and perpetuates that spirit and, which is still more important, places the higher officials of the state and communal civil administration, as well as those of the law and educational system, almost without an exception under military discipline, subjecting them to the militaristic spirit, to the whole militaristic view of life, and thus stifling in them in advance any inconvenient impulse of opposition that might possibly arise even in their official minds.(54) By these means the tractableness of the civil executive is secured, an object reached in regard to the subalterns and lower officials by means of the systems giving preference to the claims of former military persons to public posts. Provision is thus made that class justice and the class educational system shall bear their proper military stamp and that self government (55) shall be kept back with a firm hand. Also worthy of mention is the order that officers, whether in active service or not, must not do any literary work, which, alongside the highly instructive Gädke (56) case, is the most conclusive symptom of the reckless desire of militarism for intellectual subjection and the centralized supervision of everything within its reach, and also indicates its tendency continually to extend its sphere of influence, legally or illegally, its desire for unlimited growth, its unlimited appetite for power.

## OTHER WAYS OF INFLUENCING THE CIVILIAN POPULAION IN A MILITARY DIRECTION

An even more important result of the militaristic hunger for expansion than the mischievous reserve-officer system is the nuisance of the military claimant system in public employment, which, besides the purely military purpose mentioned, serves in no less a degree the purpose of sending into all the branches~of the state and municipal administration a band of always faithful and enthusiastic representatives and propagandists of the militarist tic spirit. By this method it is intended at the same time to insure the trustworthiness and loyalty of the bureaucracy serving capitalism, and to spread among the mass of the *people* who are particularly in need of education the "right," "state conserving" way of thinking. That "educational" purpose of the system was avowed with touching unanimity and frankness by Chancellor Caprivi and the representatives of the ruling classes in the Reichstag debates on the premiums for non-commissioned officers, in February, 1891. Thus, after the corporal had to leave the teacher's desk, the conservative ideal of our popular educational system has fortunately arrived again by a devious route at the non-commissioned officer.(57)

True, the educational results are very meagre ones. The poor fellows with their military claims for subordinate positions are too badly paid. After all, even a German non-commissioned officer is not to be had indefinitely for a pittance and the honor of serving the King of Prussia.(58) It is the eternal problem of buying up the revolution !

In this connection it should be mentioned that the same methods which are employed to arouse and to keep alive the military enthusiasm of the soldiers themselves, as, for instance, all the display and pomp, likewise influence the *non-military population*, i.e., those elements 'from whose ranks the army is recruited, who form its background, who have to bear its expense and who are in "danger" of falling a prey to the interior foe. The British secretary for war, Mr. Haldane, proved himself an apt pupil on his Prussian visit in the fall of ~906, when he learned that. He expressed the thought that a valuable secondary effect of militarism was that it educated the people in sobermindedness and faithfulness to duty by ' bringing them into closer contact with the army and war preparations.

*Militarism* possesses still another means, but one of quite a different kind, to spread its spirit, viz., in its character as a *consumer* and *producer* and in its influence over great industrial undertakings of the state which are of strategical importance.

Quite a host of manufacturers, tradesmen and merchants, with their employees, live by the army, people who take part in the production and the transportation of all commodities necessary for its equipment, lodging and maintenance, and of all articles of consumption needed by the soldiers. These beneficiaries of the army often positively determine the character of the whole public life of a place, especially in small garrison towns, and the most powerful among them rule like princes over large communities and play the first fiddle in their state and in the empire. They owe their influence to militarism which allows itself to be fleeced and bamboozled by them with astonishing patience, and return thanks (one good turn deserves another) by becoming its most fervent propagandists, for which part they are, of course, already cut out by their capitalist interests. Who does not know the names of Krupp, Stumm, Ehrhardt, Löwe, Wörmann, Tippelskirch, Nobel, Powder Trust, etc. — Who has not heard of Krupp's usurious rates for armor plate, of the Tippelskirch profits with the bribes appertaining to them, of the exorbitant freight and demurrage charges of Wörmann, the net 100 and 150 percent. profit of the Powder Trust which lightened the purse of the German Empire by many a million? In Austria the frauds of the army contractors have been especially sensational. And every campaign means for that parasitic crowd (not only in Russia) a golden fraudulent harvest. These mighty gentlemen, as was said before, repay militarism like true Christians for allowing them to rob it, or rather the people. They pour out the holy ghost of militarism over "their" workers and all that are dependent on them, and conduct a relentless war against the forces of revolution. Of course, neither the workmen nor the great majority of the *small* army contractors have a real material interest in the army. The countries that have no standing army are certainly not inferior in general well-being and prosperity of commerce and industry to the countries possessing a standing army, and the persons employed in the branches of military production certainly would not be worse off economically if there were no army. But as a rule they do not see beyond their nose and submit only too readily to the strong militaristic influence, so that an oppositional propaganda meets with great difficulties.

As an employer in great industrial undertakings (such as military store-houses, canning factories, clothing factories, remount-depots, arms and munition factories, navy yards, etc.) militarism does not only willingly and exclusively hand over its employees (on October 31, 1904, there were altogether 54,723 persons employed in industrial establishments owned by the administration of the German army and navy) to all reactionary patriotic demagogues, as, for example, the imperial anti-socialist union, it also attempts to permeate them systematically and ruthlessly with the patriotic militaristic spirit, by bestowing titles and decorations on them, arranging for them festivals in the manner of the veterans' associations, promising them impossible pensions, by outlawing the trade union and introducing into its shops a veritable barracks discipline. Among the government work-shops the shops of the military administration present the hardest problem in the campaign for the enlightenment of the proletariat. There is naturally a limit to the influence exercised by the forces hostile to the labor movement, and it can hardly be that the administration of the army still cherishes any illusions in view of the Social Democratic successes, especially among the workers at the imperial navy yards. The very childish threat to close down the military shops in case the Social Democratic vote among the workers should in crease, a threat employed at Spandau during the election of 1903, can impede the spreading of class-consciousness as little as any other threat, so long as militarism by giving its workers niggardly proletarian pay makes them over to the Social Democracy. One need but recall the frequent wage movements in the royal factories, the numerous conflicts of the men employed there with the military administration, conflicts which often assume an animated form, in order to overcome one's pessimism in regard to these workers.

The railroads, the postal and telegraphic services are institutions of decisive strategical importance, not only for the war against the exterior, but also for the war against the interior enemy. Those indispensable strategical factors can be made useless for militarism by a strike, which would lead to a complete paralysis of the military organism. It is therefore quite natural that militarism should earnestly strive to imbue with its spirit the minds of the officials and workmen be. longing to the staffs of those industries of communication and the factories connected with them (railroad-shops, car factories, etc.). The unscrupulous manner in which this purpose is being pursued is not only demonstrated by the system of military claimants for civil employment, previously described, but also by the fact that in several states those employees have been placed under the military law, it is further shown by their political condition, in the militarist countries where they have been deprived of the right of combination either by administrative procedure (as in Ger many and France) or by special laws (as in Italy, Holland, and also Russia). Naturally, we do not deny that apart from those military interests the capitalist state guards its general interests in preventing its employees in those industries of communication from being captured by its enemies. Those efforts, too, will necessarily be fruitless in the long run, however great the difficulties they prepare for the labor movement. They fail on account of inadequate wages, on account of the positively proletarian mode of existence of the employees of the communication systems.

## MILITARISM AS MACHIAVELLISM AND A POLITCAL REGULATOR

Militarism thus appears in the first place in *the army itself,* then as a system reaching *beyond the army and embracing all of society* in a net of militaristic and semi-militaristic institutions (such as the control system, the prohibition of literary activity, court of honor, the reserve-officer system, the provision for time-expired non-commissioned officers, the militarization of the whole bureaucratic apparatus [due above all to the mischievous reserve-officer system and the military claimants for public positions], cadet corps, veterans' associations, etc.), further as a *system of saturating the whole private and public life of our people with the military spirit* for which purpose the church, the schools, and a certain venal art' as well as the press, a despicable literary crowd and the social prestige, with which our "splendid war army" is ever being surrounded as by a *halo,* cooperate in a tenacious and cunning fashion. By the side of the Catholic Church militarism represents the acme of Machiavellism in the world's history and the most Machiavellian among all the Machiavellian institutions of capitalism.

The exploit of the Köpenick cobbler-captain, previously mentioned, may be regarded as a compendium of that whole militaristic art of education and its results, the most sublime of which is the veritable canonization of the officer's coat by the whole bourgeois society. In an examination, lasting six hours, to which this jail-bird subjected a sample of our army, our bureaucratic apparatus and the allegiance of the Prussian subject, all these probationers passed with such great honors that even their teachers were speechless with astonishment at that quintessence of their pedagogy. No Gessler's hat has ever found such willing submission and self-humiliation as the cap of the immortal Captain of Köpenick, no holy coat of Trèves has ever been worshipped so religiously as his unit form. That classical satire whose enormous effectiveness consists in its having hunted to death militarism's own pedagogic principles, ought to hunt to death militarism amidst the scornful laughter of the world if — yes, if that same bourgeois society, which in regard to militarism now finds itself for the moment in the position of the sorcerer's apt prentice who evoked the spirits but could not get rid of them, did not need militarism as badly as its daily bread and the air it breathes. The same old tragical conflict. Capitalism and its powerful major-domo, militarism, do not love each other at all, but rather fear and hate each other, for which they have many a reason; they look upon each other (for the major-domo has acquired sufficient independence) only as a necessary evil, for which again they have many a reason. The lesson of Köpenick which bourgeois society can not turn to its profit will therefore only remain a convincing argument for anti-militarist propaganda, for the Social Democracy which flourishes all the more the more militarism pushes its principles to their extreme conclusions.

What the Captain of Köpenick means for militarism in the domain of practical swindling, the inimitable Gustav Tuch was for it in the domain of honest theorizing, towards the end of the eighties. In his bulky volume, "The Expanded German Military State in its Social Significance," he sketched a future society of which the all illuminating, warming, directing central sun is militarism, its heart and soul, the only true "national and civilized socialism", where the whole state is trans. formed into the image of the barracks, the barracks being grammar school, high-school and a factory for producing patriotic spirit, the army an all comprising organization of strike-breakers. That ecstatic hallucination about the millennium of militarism was indeed mere methodical madness, but the very fact that it was a *methodical* madness, which imagined the militaristic aims and methods apart from all checks and carried them to their extreme conclusions, lends to it a symptomatic significance.

At least in one sphere of prime importance militarism, as will be shown more conclusively later on, is to-day already the central sun around which move the solar systems of class legislation, bureaucracy, police rule, class-justice and the clericalism of all denominations. It is the ultimate, some times recondite, sometimes patent regulator of all class politics, all tactics of the class-struggle, not only for the capitalist classes, but also for the proletariat, in regard to its economic organization no less than in regard to its political organization.

IV

## CONCERNING SOME CARDINAL SINS OF MILITARISM.

### MALTREATMENT OF SOLDIERS OR MILITARISM AS A REPENTANT, YET UNREFORMED SINNER.

The militarists are not all dull-witted. That is proven by the extremely clever educational system they have introduced. With noteworthy skill they rely upon mass psychology. The army of Fredericks composed of mercenaries and the scum of the population, had to be kept together for its mechanical tasks by pipe-clay drill and thrashings. That is no longer possible in an army formed on the basis of a civic duty and placing much greater demands upon the individual. This was clearly recognized at once by men like Scharnhorst and Gneisenau, (59) whose army reorganization began with the proclamation of the "freedom of the back." Yet, bad treatment, brutal insults, beatings and all kinds of cruel maltreatment belong also to the stock-in-trade of our present system of military education.

The attitude of military circles toward the maltreatment of soldiers is naturally not determined by considerations of ethics, civilization, humanity, justice, Christianity and other fine things, but purely by jesuitical expedients. The hidden danger which that maltreatment constitutes for the discipline and the "spirit" of the army itself (60) has not even to-day been generally recognized.(61) The ragging of new recruits and recalcitrants by the older men, the brutal barracks jokes and vulgar language of all kind, and the fairly frequent knocks and blows and hazing, are heartily apt proved without scruple and are even positively considered necessary by the majority of non-commissioned officers and even officers, who, estranged from and hostile to the people, have been trained to become the most narrow-minded petty despots. The fight against those outrages therefore meets almost at the outset, with an all but insuperable passive resistance. Privately, but not publicly, one may hear daily how superiors describe the desire for decent treatment of the "fellows" as a symptom of a silly humanitarian soft-headedness. Military service is a rude business. But even where they have thoroughly recognized the hidden dangers of disciplinary maltreatments they find themselves again in face of one of those disagreeable alternatives at which a system based on brute force and setting itself against the natural development must always arrive, and several of which we have already pointed out. For those maltreatments are indeed (as we shall show more conclusively) indispensable auxiliaries of the external drill which capitalist militarism, (for which the inward voluntary discipline is an unattainable goal), can not dispense with for want of a better method. We repeat that they are considered, not officially, it is true, but semi-officially, in spite of all the scruples and regrets we hear expressed, not as a legal, but as an indispensable means of military education.

But apart from military scruples, our militarists suffer from a bad conscience since they have been caught at their game, i.e., since the relentless Social Democratic criticism of the army institutions began and large portions of the middle-class commenced to disavow that military morality. With a gnashing of teeth militarism had to acknowledge that it was not simply devised and commanded by the supreme war lord, but that it depends, especially in regard to its material existence, on the popular representative body on which it looks with such scornful disdain —on the Reichstag which includes even representatives of the "mob"; in short, that it depends on the "rabble" and that under cover of their immunity the people's representatives in the Reichstag pitilessly exposed its nakedness again and again. In sullen rage it saw itself obliged to maintain the good mood of those plebeians, those Reichstag fellows, that despised and derided "public opinion." The problem was, not to put to too hard a test the devout belief in militarism possessed by the bourgeoisie who, as a rule, were ready to grant all possible military demands but who, especially in times of financial troubles, were not rarely apt to kick against the pricks, moreover, things had to be made easier for the bourgeoisie when the latter were dealing with their voters, largely anti-militarists, because of their social position, and ready to embrace Social Democracy when they recognize their class interests. Such weapons as were likely to be most effective had to be withheld or snatched from Social Democratic propagandists, so militarism had recourse to the tactics of hushing-up and concealment. The procedure of the military courts was secret, not a ray penetrated that darkness, and if one succeeded in penetrating it things were denied, disputed and extenuated with might and main. But the torch of Social Democracy sent its light farther and farther, even to behind the barracks walls and through the bars of the military prisons and fortresses. The military debates that took place in the German Reichstag in the eighties and nineties of the last century constitute a tenacious and passionate fight for the recognition of the fact that the atrocities of the barracks are not rare and isolated phenomena but regular, extraordinarily frequent, organic, constitutional occurrences, as it were, in military life. In that fight effective service was rendered by the publicity of the procedure of military courts in other countries, proving that military maltreatment is a regular attribute of militarism, even of republican militarism in France, even of Belgian militarism, even in a growing degree of the Swiss militia militarism.

The impression created by the army orders of Prince George of Saxony (of June 8, 1891 ), which were published by the *Vorwarts* at the beginning of 1892, and by the orders of the Bavarian war minister( December 13, 1891 ), and by the Reichstag debates, which lasted from February 15 to 17, 1892, was mainly responsible for the effect which the Social Democratic criticism exercised. After the usual "due considerations,, and scufflings the reform of our procedure in military trials was brought about in 1898 with a great amount of painful exertion. True, the reformed procedure still permitted the courts to a large extent to exclude the public and thus to cover the terrible secrets of the barracks with the cloak of Christian charity, but it succeeded (in spite of all the orders which almost suggested the most sweeping use of the powers of excluding the public and in spite of the much discussed disciplining of the judges in the Bilse case) in bringing down such a hail of appalling cases of maltreatment upon the heads of the public that all objections against the Social Democratic criticism were simply swept away, and the existence of the maltreatment of soldiers as a settled institution of "state-conserving" militarism was acknowledged almost everywhere, however reluctantly. More or less honestly the authorities attempted to grapple with this repelling institution which proved of too great an advantage to the socialist propaganda, and though they did not believe in any substantial success, they yet wanted to arouse the impression of dislike for the institution and readiness to try their best to abolish it. They began to hunt down with a certain amount of severity those guilty of maltreating soldiers, but militarism has after all a greater interest in maintaining military discipline, in training the people in arms to be docile fighters in the struggle against their own international and national interests than in attacking the maltreatment of soldiers. It is instructive to compare the sentences passed upon the basest tormentors of soldiers with those pronounced almost daily upon soldiers for often quite petty offences against their superiors, or for of fences committed in a state of excitement or intoxication by soldiers against their superiors. For the soldier there is a blood-thirsty, Draconic punishment for the smallest sin against the holy ghost of militarism; for the other offender there is, in spite of all, a relatively mild indulgence and understanding. Thus the campaign of the military courts against the maltreatment of soldiers, conducted parallel with a campaign to throttle every vestige of an impulse on the part of the subordinate to exhibit a consciousness of self-dependence or equality, naturally fails of practical result. The whole story is told by the case of the Hereditary Prince of Saxe-Meiningen who had sufficient courage to call upon the men themselves to assist in the campaign against maltreatment so as to be able to attack the evil more energetically than ever before at the root. He was, however, soon forced to quit the army on account of this bold step. The incident brightly illuminates the whole uselessness and hopelessness of the official campaign against the maltreatment of soldiers.

The little book written by our comrade Rudolf Krafft, a former officer of the Bavarian army, on "The Victims of the Barracks" treats valuable material with the expert knowledge that can only come from inside information. Regular compilations of trials for maltreating soldiers (or sailors), made by the Socialist press at certain intervals, furnish a positively overwhelming mass of material which has unfortunately not yet been edited. An important and thankful task is awaiting some one.

Being fundamentally opposed to militarism we have no delusions about it. Scharnhorst, in his "Order Concerning Military Punishments," writes: "Experience teaches that recruits can be taught the drill without beating them. An officer to whom this may appear impossible lacks the necessary faculty of instruction or has no clear idea of training." Of course, theoretically he is right, but practically he is far in advance of the times. The maltreatment of soldiers springs from the very essence of capitalist militarism. A large proportion of the men is intellectually, a still larger proportion physically, not equal to the military requirements, especially not equal to those of the parade drill. The number of the young men having a view of life that is dangerous and hostile to militarism, who enter the army increases continually. The problem is to tear that soul out of those "fellows," as it were, and replace it by a new patriotic soul, loyal to the king. Even the most skilful pedagogue finds it impossible to solve all those problems, let alone the land of teachers available to militarism, which must in this respect, too, be more economical than it would like to be.

The militaristic pedagogues have but a precarious subsistence. They depend entirely on the good will, on the arbitrariness of their superior, and must expect every minute to be thrown out of employment if they do not accomplish their chief task, that of forming the soldier in the image of militarism — an excellent expedient to make the whole apparatus of the military hierarchy extremely pliant in the hands of the supreme command. It goes without saying that such superiors drill their men with a nervous lack of consideration, that they soon come to the point where they use force. instead of persuasion and example, and that such force, owing to the absolute power which the superior has over the life and death of his subordinate who has to submit to him unconditionally, is finally applied in the shape of maltreaments. All this is a natural and, humanly speaking, necessary concatenation in which the new Japanese militarism, too, has promptly got entangled. It is another dilemma of militarism.

The causes of such maltreatments are not to be met with everywhere in a uniform degree. It is above all the degree of popular education which exercises a strongly modifying influence, and it is not surprising that even French colonial militarism forms in this respect a favorable contrast to the Prussian-German home militarism.

It is exactly in this form of exercising disciplinary power, and just in that necessity by which it arises out of the system, that we Socialists find an excellent weapon with which to combat militarism fundamentally and most successfully, arousing against it an ever growing portion of the people and carrying class-consciousness into groups that otherwise could not yet be reached or could only be reached with much greater difficulty. The maltreatment of soldiers and military class-justice, one of the most provoking phenomena of capitalist barbarism, are not only dangerously undermining military discipline, they are also the most effective weapons in the war for the liberation of the proletariat. That sin of capitalism turns against capitalism itself in two ways. However much the sinner may repent, honestly in helpless contrition, or in the style of the fox in the fable, those weapons can not be taken away from us; for though he appears in sackcloth and ashes the sinner is irreclaimable.

## THE COSTS OF MILITARISM OR LA DOULOUREUSE. ANOTHER DILEMMA

Historical materialism, the doctrine of dialectical evolution, is the doctrine of the inherent necessity of retribution. Every society divided in classes is condemned to commit suicide. Every society divided in classes is a force that ever wills the evil and accomplishes the good and, even if it did not will the evil, must do the evil; it must perish through the original sin of its class character; it must, whether it wants to or not, beget the OEdipus who will slay it one day, but, unlike the fabled Theban, with the full consciousness of committing parricide. That is at least true with regard to the capitalist order of society, with regard to the proletariat. Of course, the ruling class of capitalism, too, would very much like to enjoy its profits in complete comfort and security. But since that comfort and security neither agree with the national and international capitalist competition nor with the permanent taste of those at whose expense it lives, capitalism erects for the protection of wage slavery round the sanctum of profit a cruel fortress of despotism, bristling with arms. Though militarism be a vital necessity of capitalism, the latter is naturally not pleased with the gigantic expense of militarism and considers it at heart as a very disagreeable burden. However, as it is impossible today to follow the old Cadmean recipe of sowing dragon's teeth in order to make the ground yield armed soldiers, there is nothing to be done but putting up with Moloch Militarism and feeding its insatiable appetite. The annual financial debates in the various parliaments demonstrate how painful a subject this quality of militarism is to the ruling classes. Capitalism, hungering for surplus value, can only be impressed by touching the financial spot, its constitutional weak spot. The expense of militarism is the only thing that keeps it in bounds, at least as far as it is borne by the bourgeoisie itself. The ethics of profiteering, however, seeks and finds a way out that is as easy as it is base — the shifting of the greatest or a great part of the military burdens to the shoulders of those parts of the population that are not only the weakest, but for whose oppression and torture militarism is chiefly established. Like the ruling classes of other social orders the capitalist classes use their despotism, which is moreover based in the first place on the exploitation of the proletariat, not only in order to make the oppressed and exploited classes forge their own chains, but also to make them pay for themselves for those chains to as large an extent as possible. Not content with fuming the sons of the people into the executioners of the people they press the executioners' pay as much as possible out of the sweat and blood of the people. And though here and there one is sensible of the bitterly provoking effect of that infamous outrage, capitalism remains true to its faith unto death, its faith in the golden calf. To be sure, that shifting of the military burdens on to the shoulders of the poorer classes diminishes the possibility of exploiting those classes. That can not be explained away, and that likewise contributes to the annoyance of capitalism, ever intent on exploitation, at Moloch.

Militarism rests like a leaden weight on our whole life. It is particularly, however, a leaden weight for our economic life, a nightmare under which our *economic* life is groaning, a vampire sucking its blood, because it withdraws the best energies of the people from production and the works of civilization continually, year after year (In Germany there are at the moment of writing 655,000 of the strongest and most productive men, mostly between the ages of 20 and 22, permanently in the army and navy), and also because of its insane direct costs. In Germany the military and naval budget, which is increasing by leaps, amounted in the year 1906-07 (inclusive of the colonial budget, but exclusive of the supplementary estimates) to more than 1,300,000,000 marks, say one billion and a third.(62) The costs to the other military states are relatively not smaller,(63) and the military expenditure of even richer countries, such as the United States, Great Britain (which, in 1904-05, had an army and navy budget of 1,321,000,000), Belgium and Switzerland, is so extraordinary that it occupies a dominating position in the budgets of those countries. Everywhere the tendency is in the direction of a boundless increase, close to the limits of the ability to pay.

The following interesting compilation is found in the *Nouveau Manuel du soldat:*

| | |
|---|---|
| "In 1899 Europe had a military budget of | 7,184,321,093 francs. |
| It employed in a military capacity | 4, 169,321 men, |
| who, if they were to work, could produce, at the rate of three francs per day per man, the value of | 12,507,963 francs a day. |
| Europe further used for military purposes | 710,342 horses |

| | |
|---|---|
| which, at a rate of two francs per day per horse, could produce a value of | 1,420,684 francs a day. |
| Adding that sum to the 12,507,963 francs we obtain a total of | 13,928,647 francs. |
| Multiplied by 300 that sum shows, together with the budget, a lost productive value of | 11,915,913 francs." |

But in Germany alone the military budget increased from 1899 to 1906-07 from 920,000,000 to about 1,300,000,000, more than 40 percent. For the whole of Europe the total amount of military "overhead charges," not counting the costs of the Russo-Japanese War, reaches at the moment of writing some

13,000,000,000 marks per annum,

say 13 percent. of the total foreign trade of the world. In truth a veritable policy of bankruptcy!

In the Russian Baltic provinces the military suppression of the revolutionary movement was for a long time confided to the very barons affected by that movement. In a similar manner America has realized the "unlimited possibility" of leaving the maintenance of capitalist order even in times of peace to the employers, as a concession to be exploited, as it were. Thus, the Pinkertons have fairly become a legal institution for the class-struggle. At all events, that institution, like its Belgian counterpart, the civic guard, has the advantage of reducing those effects of militarism which are disagreeable even to the bourgeoisie (maltreatment of soldiers, expense, etc.) and of partly withholding some highly effective material for agitation from the enemies of the capitalist order of society. However, as has been explained, that way out of the difficulty, which is moreover anything but pleasant for the proletariat, is as a rule blocked to the capitalist countries, and the introduction of the much less burdensome militia system is for a predeterminable time denied them because of the function the army has to perform at home in the class-struggle, a function which is even developing a pronounced feeling in favor of the abolition of the existing militias.

Comparing the entire budget of the *German Empire* for 190~6-7, which amounted to 2,397,394,000 marks, with that portion of it devoted to the army and navy, we notice that all the other items play only the part of small satellites to that mighty sum, that the entire fiscal system, the entire financial system group themselves round the military budget — "as the host of the stars are mustered round the sun," as the poet says.

Hence militarism dangerously impedes, and often makes impossible even such progress in civilization as in itself would advance the interest of the existing social order. Education, art and science, public sanitation, the communication system: all are treated in a niggardly fashion since there is nothing left for works of civilization after gluttonous Moloch has been fed. The ministerial declaration that the obligations of civilization (64) did not suffer, convinced at most the East Elbian junkers with their low cultural demands whilst it could not wring more than an indulgent smile from the other representatives of capitalist society. Figures furnish the proof. It suffices to compare the one billion and a third of the German military budget of 1906 with the 171 millions that Prussia spent for all kinds of educational purposes, or the 420 millions that Austria spent for military purposes in 1900 with the 5 1/2 millions she spent for elementary education. The latest Prussian school maintenance law, with its niggardly settlement of the question of teachers' salaries, and the notorious Studt decree against the raising of teachers' salaries in the cities speak volumes.

Germany should be rich enough to fulfil all her tasks of civilization, and the more completely these tasks should be performed the easier it would be to bear their costs. But the barrier of militarism obstructs the road.

Quite especially provoking is the way in which the expenses of militarism are defrayed in Germany — and elsewhere, in France, for instance. It can almost be said that militarism is the creator and preserver of our oppressive, unjust system of indirect taxation. The entire tariff and taxation system of the Empire, which amounts to a squeezing-out of the masses, i.e., the great needy mass of our population, and to which is due, for example, that in 1906 the cost of living for the mass of the people rose by no less than from 10 to 15 percent. as against the average for the period from 1900 to 1904, not only benefits the junkers (that parasitic class so tenderly cared for, very largely for militaristic reasons), but serves in the first line militaristic purposes. It is no less mainly the fault of militarism if our system of communication, the development and perfection of which is especially to the greatest advantage of a sensible capitalism equipped with a shrewd understanding of its interests, does not by far meet the demands of traffic and technical progress, but is used as a milch-cow for a special indirect taxation of the people. The story of the Stengel bill on imperial finances ought to make even a blind man see. It is possible to calculate almost to a cent that this bill was only caused by the necessity of stopping that 200-million hole which militarism had once again succeeded in making in the imperial treasury; and the kind of taxation resorted to, which presses heavily on articles of popular consumption, beer, tobacco, etc., and even on communication, that breath of life of capitalism, excellently illustrates what was said above.

No doubt, in many respects militarism is a burden to capitalism itself, but that burden is as firmly installed on the capitalist back as the mysterious strong old man was on the shoulders of Sin bad the Sailor. Capitalism is in need of militarism just as spies are needed in times of war and executioners and their assistants in times of peace. It may hate militarism, but it can not do without it, just as the civilized Christian may detest the sins against the Gospel, but can not live without them. Militarism is one of the original sins of capitalism, which may be susceptible of being mitigated here and there, but of which it will be purged only in the purgatory of Socialism.

## THE ARMY AS A WEAPON AGAINST THE PROLETARIAT IN THE ECONOMIC STRUGGLE

### Preliminary Remarks.

We have seen that militarism has become the centre round which our political, social and economic life tends to move more and more, that it is the wire-puller operating the marionettes of the capitalist puppet-show. We have seen what the purpose is that militarism pursues, how it tries to accomplish that purpose and how in the pursuit of that end it must necessarily produce the poison by which it is to die. We have also pointed out what an important rôle as a conservative force it plays — alas! with little success — as a school for drumming proper views into the nation in uniform and civilian dress. But militarism is not content with that part; it exercises even today and in quiet times its conserving influence in various other directions, as a preparation, as a preliminary practice for the great day when after a long apprenticeship and service as a journeyman it has to produce its masterpiece, for the day when the people rises boldly and fearlessly against its rulers, the day of the great reckoning.

On that day, which the elect of militarism would see dawn rather today than tomorrow (because they hope that the sooner it comes the more surely it will be the deluge of Social Democracy) militarism will shoot, fire grape-shot and massacre *en masse* to its heart's content "with God, for King and Fatherland." The 22nd of January, 1905, the bloody May week of 1871 will be its ideal and model. The commander of the Vienna corps, Schonfeldt, made a touching vow at a banquet oú feasting bourgeois in April, 1894, when he said: "I can assure you that you, too, will find us behind your front when the existence of society, the enjoyment of the hard earned property are endangered. When the citizen stands in the first line the soldier flies to his assistance."

Thus the mailed fist is ever raised and ready to come down with a crushing blow. Hypocritically they speak about "the maintenance of law and order," "the protection of the liberty to work," and mean "the maintenance of oppression," "the protection of exploitation." Whenever the proletariat exhibits an inconvenient animation and power, militarism at once attempts to scare it back by the rattling of the sabre, that militarism which, ever present and omnipotent, is behind every action the forces of the state undertake against the forces of labor, and gives to such action the ultimate, still invincible weight. That weight is, however, not merely reserved, behind the vanguard of the police and constabulary, for important occasions, but is also constantly available for the clearly understood purpose of aiding in the everyday work and of strengthening in a sustained guerilla warfare the pillars of the capitalist society. It is just that restlessly and craftily employed versatility that characterizes capitalist militarism.

## SOLDIERS AS THE COMPETITORS OF FREE WORKERS

As a functionary of capitalism militarism fully understands that its greatest and most sacred task is that of increasing the profits of the employing class. Thus it thinks itself authorized and even obliged to place the soldiers, officially or semi-officially, as beasts of burden at the disposal of employers, particularly the junkers, who use the soldiers to supply that want of farm hands which has been caused by the inhuman exploitation and brutal treatment of the farm laborers.

To send *soldiers to help with the harvest* is a practice as constantly met with as it is detrimental and inimical to the interests of labor. It reveals, like the system of soldier-servants, (65) the whole mischievous and stupid humbug behind the arguments which are used by those monomaniacs of the goosestep and the parade drill to show the purely military necessity of a long period of military service, and awakens not very flattering reminiscences of the company system of the time before the crash of Jena. More complicated are the numerous cases in which the post office and the railroad management temporarily employ soldiers at times of heavy traffic, but they should also be mentioned in this connection.

## THE ARMY AND STRIKE-BREAKING

By sending soldiers under military command *to act as strike-breakers* militarism interferes directly with the struggle of labor to emancipate itself. We need only point to the case of the present com mender of the Imperial Anti-socialist Union, Lieutenant-General v. Liebert, who even as a simple colonel had comprehended in 1896 that strikes are a calamity, like a conflagration or inundation, of course, a calamity for the employers whose protecting spirit and executive officer he felt himself to be.

As regards Germany, a special notoriety attaches to the method of gently pushing the men released from military service into the ranks of the strike-breakers, a method practiced as late as the summer of 1906 during the Nuremberg strike.

Of much greater importance are three events that occurred outside of Germany. In the first place we must mention the military strike-breaking on a large scale that took place during the Dutch general railroad strike in January, 1903, and which had its crowning achievement in the law withdrawing from the railroad workers the right to organize. In the second place we refer to the military strike-breaking on a large scale during the general strike of the Hungarian railroad workers in 1904, on which occasion the military administration went farther still and not only commanded the men in active military service to break the strike, illegally keeping them with the colors beyond their period of service, but had the impudence to mobilize the railroad workers of the first and second reserves and such other men of the military reserves as had the necessary technical equipment, and force them into strike-breaking service on the railroad under military discipline. Finally, military strike-breaking on a large scale was resorted to during the Bulgarian railroad strike which was proclaimed on January 3, 1907. Of no less importance is the campaign inaugurated at the beginning of the month of December, 1906, in Hungary by the minister for agriculture in conjunction with the minister of war against the right of combination and the strikes of agricultural laborers, in which campaign stress was laid upon the desirability of thoughtfully training soldiers to serve as bands of strike-breakers in harvest-time.

In France, too, strike-breaking by soldiers is well-known.

The fact that military education systematically fosters strike-breaking propensities and that the workmen released from the active army become dangerous to the struggling proletariat, on account of their readiness to attack the members of their own class in the rear, must also be counted among the international militaristic achievements.

## THE RULE OF THE SABRE AND GUN IN STRIKES

*Preliminary Remarks.*

Military authorities everywhere have always been convinced of the capitalist truth of the saying that the *Hydra of revolution* is lurking behind every strike. The army is therefore always ready to put to flight with sabre and gun the disobedient slaves of the capitalist whenever the fists, sabres and pistols of the police are not immediately effective in so-called strike riots. That is true in regard to all the capitalist countries and also, of course, in the highest degree of Russia, which, as a whole, is not yet a capitalist country, and which can not be considered as typical in this respect on account of special political and cultural conditions. Though Italy and Austria are among the greatest sinners, they are surpassed by the states enjoying a republican or semi-republican form of government. In judging historically the value of the republican form of government under the capitalist economic system it is of the greatest importance to point out persistently that, apart from England, there were no countries where the soldiery was so willing to suppress strikes for the benefit of the employers and behaved so bloodthirstily and recklessly as the republican or semi-republican countries, like Belgium and France, with which the freest countries of the world, Switzerland and America, can easily bear comparison. Russia is, of course in this respect, as in all spheres of cruelty, beyond comparison. Barbarism and worse than barbarism — the savageness of the beast characterizes the general civilization of her ruling classes and is the natural inclination of her militarism, which has literally bathed itself, ever since the first timid stirrings of the proletariat, in the blood of' peaceful workmen who in monstrous misery vlere crying for deliverance. One must not cite any particular event, as that would mean tearing in a petty and arbitrary spirit a link out of an endless chain. For every drop of proletarian blood that has been shed in the economic struggle in all the other countries taken together, Czarism has crushed a proletarian body, in order to suppress the most modest beginnings of a labor movement.

An employment of military power similar in its nature we observe in the activities of the colonial armies and constabularies against those natives of the colonies who will not willingly allow themselves to be brought under the yoke of the meanest exploitation and greed. However, we can not deal more fully with this particular subject.

It must still be mentioned that often no sharp distinction can be made in this connection between the army proper and the constabulary and the police; they work together intimately, they replace and supplement one another and belong closely together, if for no other reason than that the quality which counts here — a violent combative temper, a willingness and readiness to sabre the people resolutely and ruthlessly, is also, in the case of the police and constabulary, mainly a genuine product of the barracks, a fruit of military education and training.

## Italy.

In two instructive articles (published in *Mouvement Socialiste*, May-June and August-September, 1906, *Les massacre de classe en Italia*) Ottavio Dinale gives an historical account of massacres of workmen in Italy. He does not merely deal with massacres directly connected with strikes, but also with those got up on occasions of labor demonstrations in the economic struggle outside of strikes. The articles show clearly how quickly the army appears on the scene in Italy on such occasions, for what slight cause and with what sur passing severity military attacks are made on defenceless crowds, how it is even customary to continue firing into and slashing at the fleeing, dispersed crowd. He sums up by stating that in Italy the "bullets of the King" shatter the bones of Italian workmen every year perhaps some five, six or even ten times. He points out that the Italian bourgeoisie, the author of those massacres, is among the most narrow-minded, backward bourgeois classes of the world, that in the eyes of these capitalists Socialism is not a political philosophy, but a species of criminal disposition, criminal propensity, the most dangerous for public order. He quotes the words written by the Milan newspaper *Idea liberale* on the morrow of the butchery of Grammichele: "Killed and wounded — those people have met the fate they deserve *the grapeshot, that is the most precious element of civilization and order.*"

After such samples one need not be astonished to hear that even a so-called democratic government, like that of Giolitti, never could be got to call the military to account for their bloodthirsty barbarities, but rather praised them officially "for having done their duty." It appears still more natural that a resolution of the Socialist party in the Italian Chamber demanding restrictive regulations in regard to the employment of the military in collective conflicts should be voted down.

The first effect of the shootings of the month of May of 1898 was to clear the situation in the class-struggle and make even the blind and the short-sighted optimists see how matters stood. The following is a nearly complete register of the bloodshed of recent years:

|  |  | killed | wounded |
|---|---|---|---|
| 1901, June 27, | Berra | 2 | 10 |
| 1902, May 4, | Patugnano | 1 | 7 |
| 1902, August 5, | Cassano | 1 | 3 |
| 1902, September 8, | Candela | 5 | 11 |
| 1902, October 13 , | Giarratana | 2 | 12 |
| 1903, May 21, | Piere | 3 | 1 |

| | | | |
|---|---|---|---|
| 1903, April 20, | Galatina | 2 | 1 |
| 1903, August 31, | Torre Annunziata | 7 | 10 |
| 1904, May 17, | Cerignola | 3 | 40 |
| 1904, September 4, | Buggera | 3 | 10 |
| 1904, September 11, | Castelluzzo | 1 | 12 |
| 1904, September 15, | Sestri Ponente | 2 | 2 |
| 1905, April 18, | Foggia | 7 | 20 |
| 1905, May 15, | St. Elpidio | 4 | 2 |
| 1905, August 16, | Grammichele | 18 | 20 |
| 1906, March 23, | Muro | 2 | 4 |
| 1906, March 21, | Scarano | 1 | 9 |
| 1906, April 30, | Calinera | 2 | 3 |
| 1906, April 4, | Turino | 1 | 6 |
| 1906, May 12, | Cagliari | 2 | 7 |
| 1906, May 21, | Nebida | 1 | 1 |

| 1906, May 21, | Sonneza | 6 | 6 |
| 1906, May 24, | Benventare | 2 | 2 |

The total number is 23 butcheries with 78 killed and 218 wounded. A good harvest!

Innumerable are the cases in Italy where the military have been mobilized against workmen and "peasants" that were on strike or were demonstrating for some economic reason and where no blood was shed. Those "exercises" of the army are daily news items on the other side of the Alps.

We may also mention here as a matter of course a fact attested by Hervé, viz., that, just as it is in Italy, it is impossible to keep pace with the butcheries of striking workmen and peasants in Spain, a country in whose territories once upon a time the sun never set and where it does not seem ever to rise nowadays.

## Austria-Hungary.

As is generally known, matters are not much better under the black and yellow flag of the Dual Monarchy. The Socialist deputy Daszynski could justly exclaim in the Austrian parliament on September 25, 1903, "During strikes and popular demonstrations, as well as during the ebullitions of national feeling it is always the army which turns its bayonets against the people, against the workmen, against the peasants." And with reference to general Austrian politics he could as justly point. out, "We live in a state in which, even in times of peace, the army remains the only thing that will cement together such disparate elements." He could point to the incidents that took place at Graz in ~897 and the blood shed at Graslitz. At the downfall of Prime Minister Badeni, in the month of November, ~897, the military were employed in Vienna, Graz and Budapest with sanguinary results. We remember the frequent butcheries of workmen in Galicia (a case deserving special notice is that in which the blood of farm laborers was shed at Burowicki and Ubinie [Kanimko], in 1902), the bloody events at Falkenau, Nürschan and Ostrau, which must properly be credited to the constabulary, a special body which is particularly devoted to maintain order in the interior and is partly subject to the orders of the military authorities, partly to those of the civil administrative authorities, which however is subject to a purely military discipline. During the general strike at Trieste, in February, 1902, there were also clashes with the army, and ten persons were either killed or wounded. We must also mention the incidents that took place during the bricklayers' strike at Lemberg in 1902, and the political demonstrations succeeding that strike, when hussars rode and shot into the crowd, killing five persons. The purely nationalistic scuffle at Innsbruck in 1905 is, however, outside the scope of our subject.

In Hungary considerable military excesses directed against the populace occurred quite frequently up to recent years, and the constabulary has always done its "full duty"; as, for instance, during the riots on the Pussta Tamasie, where it fired on peaceful farm hands without any reason whatever. One particular event of most recent date should be remembered, viz., the battle that was fought on September 2, 1906, in the county of Hunyad, where the military were on the rampage among the striking miners of the Petroseny coal mines. Numerous persons were severely wounded, two mortally, and a hundred and fifty were slightly wounded.

On a later occasion we shall briefly refer to the other skirmishes and engagements which the army has fought in the *politcal* struggles of the proletariat of the Habsburg Dual Monarchy.

In the speech mentioned above, Daszynski demanded that the *"bayonets should not mix in politics."* But since that time, as every one knows, the bayonets have turned to politics more eagerly and actively than ever before.

## Belgium.

In Belgium the butcheries of workmen have a long history. The events of the years 1867 and 1868 are of importance, if only on account of the intercession of the International. The butcheries begin with the so-called hunger revolt of Marchienne in 1867, when processions of defenceless demonstrating workmen were set upon by a company of soldiers and cut down. There followed, in the month of March, 1868, the massacre of Charleroi and, in 1869, the infamous butcheries of Seraing and the Borinage.

The massacre of Charleroi, arranged by the military and constabulary against the miners who had been driven to the utmost desperation in consequence of the restriction of output and wage reductions, induced the International at the time to begin a vigorous agitation in Belgium, and led to a proclamation by the General

Council of the International, which resulted in a considerable success for the International as regards organization.

The scenes of the sixties were repeated during the so-called hunger rebellions of 1886 in which not only economic questions, but also the demand for universal suffrage played a part, the latter in a confused manner, it is true. General Baron Vandersmissen issued his notorious circular letter on April 3,1886, a circular later condemned by even the Chamber of Deputies, in which he declared cynically, *"L'usage des armes est fait sans aucune sommation"* [use is made of arms without previous warning]. There was an unheard-of number of victims. In Raux alone 16 workmen were killed by a volley. On all this class-justice set its stamp of approval and laid particular emphasis by numerous heavy sentences which were imposed on workmen. From 1886 to 1902 there was scarcely a strike in Belgium without the military interfering. In that period some 80 men were killed. During the general strike of 1893, which though of a political nature may be mentioned in this connection, numerous people were left dead on the field of battle. The names of Verviers, Roux, La Louvière, Jemappes, Ostende, Bergerhout, Mons have been burnt as with a red-hot iron into the memory of the class-conscious Belgian working-class. They are blood-stained leaves in the big book registering the sins of Belgian capitalism. It was in 1902 that the standing army, together with the reserves, was mobilized for strike purposes for the last time, that time in consequence of the general strike. The unfavorable reports about the disposition and sentiments of the soldiers that reached the cabinet and were soon verified by the fact that the soldiers began to show their revolutionary temper in a fairly open manner, sang the Marseillaise, hissed their officers, etc., led to the Flemish soldiers being sent to the Walloon districts and vice versa, and finally brought about the decision not to use the standing army at all. Since 1902 the proletarian soldiers of Belgium have ceded the honorable role of acting the watch-dog to capitalism, the part of a "flying sen try before the money-chest of the employers," at least as far as the interior militarism is concerned, to the constabulary and civic guard, as previously set forth. To protect their sacred exploiting privileges the bourgeoisie were now at all events obliged to exert themselves and risk their own skins — if such a danger can be said to exist at all in face of unarmed crowds. Elsewhere we have described that the civic guard does excellent work in the fight against the interior enemy.

## France.

In France the history of the class-struggle has been written with rivers of blood. We will not conjure up the hecatombs of the three days' battle of July, 1830; nor the 10,000 that died in the street fighting from June 23 to 26, 1848, the victims of the executioner Cavaignac; nor the first of December, 1851, of Napoleon the "Little"; nor the sea of blood made with those 28,000 heroes, in which the French bourgeoisie, murdering in a wholesale fashion as the agent and avenger of a capitalism that was shrieking with rage, tried in the red week of May of 1871 to drown the Commune, that capitalist slave war; nor the Pere Lachaise cemetery and its wall of the Federals, the monuments of an incomparable heroism. These struggles, revolutionary in the highest degree, in which militarism did its fearful work, are outside the scope of our historical speculations.

The exploits of French militarism against defenceless striking workmen begin at an early date. The so-called "rebellion" of the silk weavers of Lyons, whose banner bore the famous and moving words, *"vivre en travaillant ou mourir en combattant"* [to live working or to die fighting, began in the month of November, 1831, by the military firing on a peaceful demonstration; in a fight lasting two days the indignant workmen conquered the town, the national guard fraternizing with them; but soon the military occupied the town without a blow. Ricamari, Saint-Aubin and Decazeville are names of localities rendered famous by the first exploits of militarism under the second French Empire. In those times the bourgeois republicans were most vehemently opposed to sending soldiers to the strike districts. These same republicans had scarcely got into power when they themselves began to adopt the method of Bonapartism which they had only just fought against, and they soon excelled their model. They found words of disapproval only when the culprit was a Clerical or a Monarchist, and then only out of political spite. At Fourmies a bullet from a Lebel rifle, striking down a young girl, Marie Blondeau, on May 1, 1891, inaugurated the new regime's baptism of blood. The bag of the day, which was made by the 145th regiment of the line, consisted of 10 killed and 35 wounded. But the butchers of Fourmies, Constant and his assistant, Captain Chapuis, were soon to have companions. Fourmies was followed by Chalons in 1899, La Martinique in 1900, then Longwy, where the officers sealed and celebrated the Franco-Russian alliance by using Russian knouts; finally, in the months of May and June, 1905, there were the events of Villefranche-sur-Saone and particularly Limoges with the cavalry charges and shootings of April 17, 1905. In December, 1905, the drama of Combree was enacted, and on January 20, 1907, the people demonstrating in favor of Sunday as a day of rest were chased off the streets of Paris by an immense muster of troops. In this recital we must also not forget Dunkirk, Creuset and Montceau-les-Mines where, according to the report made by the *Confédération Générale du Travail* (the French Federation of Labor) to the Dublin international conference, the soldiers declared their solidarity with the strikers.

What Meslier exclaimed during the latest great anti-militaristic trial is true: "Since the murder of little Marie Blondeau at Fourmies the workingclass of France has passed through a long martyrdom abounding in victims." Nothing shows better the absurdity of the illusion of a peaceful development cherished by the adherents of the"new method," than the fact that the vigorous growth and increase of anti-clerical and republican sentiment and activities which could be noticed in the France of the last five years, the France of Millerandism, has not resulted in a diminution, but positively in an increase of the "punitive expeditions", of the military against strikers. The latest radical democratic government of Clémenceau with its two Socialists will also not bring about a change. Lafargues's pointed remark in the *Humanité*, "The modern armies serve exclusively for the protection of capitalist property, in so far as they do not concern themselves with plundering colonies," hits the nail on the head in regard to France also.

### United States of America.

It is easy to show what that "tone of equality" signifies which, according to Professor Sombart, pervades in many respects the social and public life of the United States, and to demonstrate that capitalism, when it comes to the point, can very effectively reinforce its "tone" by the sound of the cannon, the rattling of musketry and the swishing of the sabre, an accomplishment in which it still outstrips even the proletariat of America. The following facts are not only instructive in regard to the great importance which the methods of military recruiting and the disposition and training of troops have for their availability against the "interior enemy. They often assume a peculiar character in consequence of the comparatively well-armed condition of the working-class, attributable to circumstances peculiar to America.

Beyond the ocean, as in Belgium, the period of the butchery of workingmen begins with the movement of the unemployed. On January 13, 1874, a strong police force pounced upon an unemployed demonstration without any provocation. Hundreds of severely wounded workmen remained on the battle-field of Tompkins Square, New York. Then followed the dramatic events of the railroad strike in the month of July, 1877. Against the strikers of the Baltimore and Ohio Railroad the governor of West Virginia sent several companies of state militia which proved too weak however. The 250 men of the Federal army sent to their aid by President Hayes achieved no better result. In Maryland the rifles of the militia killed ten and wounded a greater number of men. In Pittsburgh the local militia, called upon by the sheriff, refused to act. The old trick of employing men from other parts of the country was resorted to. Six hundred men of the militia sent from Philadelphia fought a short but fierce battle with the strikers, but were beaten and fled the next morning. The militia called out against the strikers in Reading, Pennsylvania consisted mostly of workmen who fraternized with the strikers, distributed their ammunition among them and threatened to turn their arms against all hostile militia units. But one company, which was almost exclusively composed of men belonging to the possessing classes and was led by a reckless officer, opened fire on the crowd, killing 13 and wounding 22 persons. The company was, however, given no time to enjoy its exploit, and had to retire soon in a badly beaten-up condition. St. Louis, which for a time was entirely in the hands of the strikers, was finally re-conquered for "law and order", by, the entire police force and several companies of the militia, after a veritable siege of the headquarters of the executive committee.(66)

The terror which overtook Chicago in the month of May, 1886, is attributable to the Pinkertons and the police force. Mr. McCormick, of the McCormick Reaper Works, let his armed Pinkertons loose upon the strikers (to protect the "willing workers," as was alleged), and thus started off the sanguinary attacks by the police, who clubbed men, women and children without distinction, killed six persons and wounded numerous others. That occurred on May 3. On the 4th of May the celebrated dynamite bomb affair occurred, which produced a violent street battle in which 4 workmen were killed and about 50 wounded, whilst of the police 7 were killed and 60 wounded. The whole world is acquainted with the horrible trial arising out of the events of May 4, 1886, a trial in which the democratic class-justice of America gave a splendid proof of its qualifications.

The events during the period from 1892 to 1894 deserve a more detailed treatment. In the first place, violent fights took place in the month of July, 1892, during the strike in Carnegie's iron and steel works at Homestead between the armed Pinkertons, called in by the employer; 12 men were killed and 20 severely wounded, the Pinkertons were beaten, and finally Federal troops brought about the defeat of the strikers by occupying the town, and with the help of military law. Almost at the same time a miners' strike broke out in Coeur d'Alene, Idaho. Here the militia, which was only some 100 strong, was not in a position to interfere in the fight between the strike-breakers and~the strikers, who were well armed. It was only when Federal troops, asked for by the governor, arrived that the strikers were routed.

In Buffalo the switchmen went on strike in the month of August, 1892. The local militia, called out immediately at the beginning of the strike, did not appear to be inclined to prevent picketing. Finally the sheriff was asked to request the governor to send troops, whereupon the entire militia of the state, twenty times more numerous than the strikers, appeared on the scene within forty-eight hours and restored "peace and quiet."

In the same month the strikes at the iron mines of Inman and at the coal mines of Oliver Springs and Coal Creek caused the governor of Tennessee to concentrate the whole available force of the state militia, after some portions of the militia had been disarmed by the strikers and sent home again. Here, too, the suppression of the strike was followed by the merciless work of class-justice.

Finally we must make mention of the Pullman strike of 1894, when the President of the United States, not heeding the protest of Mr. Altgeld, the governor of Illinois, despatched Federal troops who broke the strike in conjunction with the state militia; 12 men were killed. As in all the other preceding cases the courts, it is true, worked jointly with militarism and contributed so much to the defeat of the workmen by means of the famous injunctions and wholesale imprisonments that the leader of the strike, Debs, attested: "Not the railroads, not the army defeated us, but the power of the courts of the United States."

It still remains true that, though the militia failed frequently and though the strikers were frequently armed, it was the military power that decided the defeats of the workers in all the cases .mentioned, and subsequently, too, the strikers in America "were in a majority of cases quelled by the aid of the local police, state militia or Federal troops," also aided, to be sure, by "government by injunction." Almost without an exception the strikes ended thus with the defeat of the workmen, according to Hillquit, who seems to be somewhat too pessimistic in this connection.

## Canada.

Canada's "free" soil was reddened by the blood of workmen at Hamilton on November 24, 1906. During a collision with striking railroadmen the militia wounded 50 persons, some of them severely.

## Switzerland.

Switzerland's record in this field of military activity is truly quite a long one. As early as 1869 the government of Geneva employed both the police force and the militia against striking workmen. In the same year the government of the canton of Vaud recalled by telegraph a battalion that had marched off to do military exercises, supplied it with ball-cartridges and had it march with fixed bayonets into the town, where the workmen were on strike. It was also in 1869 that the government of Basle made troops act as pickets against the workers when the women silk weavers struck to improve their miserable conditions, and when in the same year a strike of vase-makers and engravers broke out at La Chaux de Fonds, the new bourgeois government provided itself with arms and ammunition for a possible mobilization of the militia.

In 1875 blood was shed. The government of the canton of Uri mobilized the militia against 2,000 striking workmen employed at the construction of the St. Gothard tunnel, who were chiefly up in arms against the shameful truck system, it is said that the employers interested placed 20,000 francs at the disposal of the government for that mobilization. As a result of the bold attack several people were killed and some 15 remained wounded on the battle-field of the class-struggle. Blood was also shed in 1901 by two companies called out against the strikers of the Simplon tunnel by the government of the canton of Valais. Some workmen were severely wounded on that occasion. In the same year two companies of the militia had to do duty as pickets against striking Italian bricklayers in the canton of

Tessino. In the month of October, 1902, occurred the well-known affair of Geneva where, during a strike directed against an American band of exploiters, the workmen were chased and clubbed by order of the government of Geneva. Militiamen who refused at the time to act as bum-bailiffs were imprisoned and declared to have forfeited their civic rights. Incidentally it may be mentioned that on that occasion even many of the bourgeois that had not been called out armed themselves against the workers. At about the same time the militia was mobilized at Basle for a strike. In 1904 the employers of the building trade at Chaux de Fonds called upon the government for military help against a strike which to their disgust was perfectly orderly in spite of all provocations and therefore hopeless from the employers' point of view; as a result, cavalry and a battalion of infantry appeared promptly on the scene and, by intimidating the proletarians who were conducting a legal fight, forced them back into capitalist slavery. It was also in 1904 that the military was called out against strikers at the Ricken, in the canton of St. Gall, to protect, as was alleged, the fruit and vegetable harvest which was in no way endangered. St. Gall also sent its militia to Rohrschach, where, during a disagreement about wages in the foundries owned by French capitalists, an excited crowd had smashed a few windowpanes. A very serious affair took place at Zurich in the summer of 1906. In consequence of the great increase in the prices of all necessaries of life several strikes for higher wages had broken out in that city, when the workmen employed in the building trades likewise proclaimed a strike for the same reason. The militia interfered without the slightest cause with sanguinary results, and beat and clubbed the striking workmen in the most brutal fashion, dragging especially the foreign strikers off to the barracks where they were struck with riding-whips under the direction of the officers. Moreover, picketing was prohibited as well as every kind of demonstration. The interpellation relating to those infamous events which was presented in the Grand Council was at first laid on the shelf and finally simply throttled without any discussion by the solid bourgeois majority. And to cap it all, six of the strike leaders were put on trial and, on August 24, 1906, Sigg was sentenced to be imprisoned for eight months and to forfeit his active civic rights for one year, for an alleged incitement to mutiny by means of an anti-militarist leaflet addressed to the militia; the other five were acquitted.

More can hardly be expected from a bourgeois republic and a militia.

These things appear in their proper significance in connection with the fact mentioned elsewhere — that the Swiss citizens not in active military service had their ammunition taken out of their custody in 1899. It will be seen that this happened just early enough to facilitate, in view of the intensified form of the class-struggle, the employment of the militia in the interests of the capitalists.

On December 21, 1906, the National Council had adopted, by a majority of 65 against 55, a clause of the law on military re-organization providing that, if conflicts of an economic nature "should endanger or disturb internal peace," the calling-out of troops "necessitated thereby" shall be resorted to solely for the purpose of *"maintaining public order."* The whole law was adopted by 105 votes against 4. Undoubtedly the provision referred to does not mean anything but what was hitherto the rule of conduct followed when the military was called out; it is thus worthless, doubly worthless, nay, positively suspicious in view of the great minority who declared themselves even against *that* clause.

## Norway.

Norway, the free country that went through the most agreeable revolution in the world's history in the summer of 1905 and then proceeded to indulge in a monarchical head for her state out of pure love of pleasure, follows entirely the development of the capitalistic countries in spite of all the rustic romanticism still clinging to her. The employment of military force against striking workmen is also no rare occurrence in that country of the peasant democracy. In an article that appeared in the *Tyvende Aarhundrede* on May 1, 1903, a report is made on the subject. We learn that in 1902 alone two cases of the kind occurred, one in Dunderlands Dalen and the other in Tromsö.

## Germany.

There remains to be considered Germany. It is just in Germany where the employment of the military in economic conflicts is not customary. Scarcely any cases in which the army interfered actively can be reported, if we except the weaver riots of 1847, when the Prussian infantry killed 11 and wounded 24 of those wretched, atrociously tortured proletarians and class-justice finished the soldiers' work by sending a great number of people to the penitentiary, and if we further except the miners' strike of 1889, when the troops called for by Provincial President von Hagemeister, on May 10, killed 3 and wounded 4 persons at the Moltke mine and killed 2 and wounded 5 in Bochum. During the riots of the Berlin unemployed, February, 1892, the military did not go into action, but it has been asserted on good authority that the Berlin military were consigned as early as January 18, 1894, on the mere rumor that the unemployed planned a demonstration before the palace in Berlin.

However, that military "moderation" does not find an explanation, as might be supposed, in a particularly mild and just disposition of the men at the helm of German affairs. The contrary is true of them. Germany possesses a strong police and constabulary force, excellently organized for rendering service to the capitalists. It is not for nothing that Germany enjoys the reputation of being the police state *par excellence*. Police and constabulary, both armed with deadly weapons, fulfil entirely the functions which elsewhere are allotted rather to the military, and in face of the greatly varying momentary requirements they prove themselves more handy and adaptable than the more clumsy and cumbrously working machinery of the army. The number of sanguinary conflicts between strikers and the police or constabulary is quite large in Germany. The strike of the Berlin street railroadmen in 1900 and the so-called Breslau riots of 1906 are by no means exceptions. Biewald's (67) hacked-off hand is only; an exceptionally provoking piece of evidence for the blindly furious recklessness of our police, that recklessness which is a fruit of military training. That hand is in goodly company alongside of split heads, amputated ears, noses, fingers and other parts of the body, and that collection is increasing rapidly. Altogether the number of cases in which blood is shed by the armed forces of the government during strikes can hardly be much lower in Germany than in other countries. To be sure it is quite impossible to estimate them even approximately as, unfortunately, the cases of people hurt by the police during strikes are not adequately registered and inefficiently heeded. But if the number of those victims should be smaller in Germany than elsewhere this is not to be credited to the good, humane intentions of the employers, of the capitalist state. That is proved most conclusively by the fact that in Germany, too, military consignations and the holding ready of troops are almost uniformly resorted to during great strikes. The gravest case in point was furnished by the great strike of the Westphalian miners which lasted from January 8 to February 10, 1905.(68)

The successful prevention of greater bloodshed should rather be exclusively ascribed to the sobermindedness, moderation and strict self-discipline, to the training and the enlightened state of mind of the German working-class. And we should not doubt that the Prussian and Saxon governments, for instance, would not think twice before coming to the assistance of capitalism in the economic conflict or a suitable occasion with rifles, sabres and guns and all the paraphernalia- of militarism.

On May 19, 1889, the German Emperor explained to the deputation the miners had sent to him: "If I should notice that Social-Democratic tendencies get mixed up with the movement and men are incited to illegal resistance I shall interfere with merciless rigor and employ the power — and it is a large one — which belongs to me." According to the *Freisinnige Zeitung* he also expressed himself thus: If the *least resistance* were offered to the authorities he would *have everybody shot down.*

## VETERANS' ASSOCIATIONS AND STRIKES.

Considering that militarism takes pains by means of veterans' associations to keep up the militaristic sentiments of the men even after they have passed out of active military service and to propagate such sentiments, it must appear almost as a matter of course that the veterans' associations also interfere in strikes. To be sure, they are not able to take an active part in the violent suppression of the economic struggles of labor, but they may yet be called predestined strike-breaking organizations. In certain places at least one would very much like to employ them for that purpose. But the full exploitation of the veterans' associations for that purpose is impeded by the following facts and considerations: that these clubs contain, in spite of all the precautions taken, a considerable percentage of oppositional and even Social Democratic elements, that it is in conflicts between capital and labor sooner than in other cases that even the most lamb-like workmen, men who are least intelligent in regard to social questions find themselves getting angry and have an appreciation of the class-struggle and the position of their own class drummed into them, and that too reckless an anti-labor policy fails in its purpose and rouses even the Catholic and Liberal labor organizations. At any rate, the discussion about this subject which took place in July, 1906, at Ostheim, at the convention of the Grandducal Saxon Veterans' and Military Association of Saxe-Weimar, is of the greatest interest. The discussion arose in connection with a principle adopted by the convention, according to which every member of the association is in duty bound to urge the expulsion of such members as are shown to be adherents of parties hostile to the government, especially of the Social Democratic party.

The result was that not all strikes, but all those strikes which run counter to the members' duty of "fidelity to Emperor, Prince and Fatherland" are considered as actions betraying sentiments hostile to the government and revolutionary sentiments. Since it will depend upon the eminent gentlemen who as a matter of course play the first fiddle in the veterans' associations, to declare where and when said fidelity is called in question by a strike, and since those gentlemen, like our police and courts, are only too much accustomed to consider strikes (which only too often touch their own vital interests, directly or indirectly) as Social Democratic machinations, we can count upon a profitable activity of the veterans' associations in that field of labor. But it will be profitable not so much for the capitalists as for the Social Democracy, to which nothing can be more welcome than such clumsy tomfoolery that can only serve to enlighten the workmen and weaken the veterans' associations. The latter are expelling more systematically than ever not only the Social Democrats, but all of their members belonging to trade unions pervaded by the spirit of the modern labor movement. In the smaller places, no doubt, they create temporary difficulties for the unions by such methods, as they hold their members not only by means of the usual parades and carousels, but also by certain material advantages which have often been acquired through the payment of considerable dues.

The activities of the veterans' associations are energetically promoted by the courts of class-justice and the administrative authorities, who still have the courage to take up the grotesque position that these clubs, which betray their political propagandist character at every turn, are to be treated as non-political organizations That is a help which those organs of the capitalist state must render militarism if only for reasons of solidarity and in the interest of the common greater purpose, the-protection of the capitalist order of society.

## THE ARMY AS A WEAPON AGAINST THE PROLETARIAT IN THE POLITICAL STRUGGLE, OR THE RULE OF THE CANNON.

Just as the political struggle is the highest, most concentrated form of the class-struggle, the direct and indirect political interference in the classstruggle by militarism, that most concentrated manifestation of political power, shows the activities of militarism in their highest, most concentrated form. In this respect militarism operates in the first place as an economic power, as a producer and consumer. The ruthless exclusion of all Social Democrats and workmen suspected of sympathizing with them from the military workshops, of Spandau, for instance, the practice of handing over the workmen subject to military influence to the absolute control of the reactionary parties, particularly to the anti-socialist union, the black hundreds of Germany, the complete isolation of those workmen from even the slightest contact with the Social Democracy: all this demonstrates how perfectly militarism has comprehended its chief task, that of protecting the capitalists, and how it performs it with professional smartness. In this respect no Krupp, no Stumm (69) is fit to hold a candle to militarism, which even surpasses those whose interests it looks after in the energetic manner in which those interests are cared for. In the military work-shops of Spandau, for instance, the influence of the anti-socialist union is such as to make that organization positively the keeper of every workman's conscience in the royal factories, and it is simply for that organization to decide whether a workman is to be dismissed. Another striking proof of that statement was furnished by the incidents connected with the dismissal of the committee of a harmless society of unskilled laborers of the military shops in the summer of 1906. A considerable influence, which is now, however, rapidly decreasing, is exercised by militarism by means of a boycott directed against all those saloon keepers whose places are used by workmen's societies or associations even slightly suspected of Social Democratic sympathies. By that boycott it kills two birds with one stone. It protects the soldiers as much as possible from coming into contact with the poison of revolution (that, by the way, is part of the chapter on military pedagogy). In the second place, it makes it harder for the workmen to procure meeting places, as the policy is often carried out systematically so as to prevent the workmen from renting any halls at all. In Berlin that kind of boycott has proved impracticable and has been nearly done away with for that reason, but our comrades in the smaller places have had no little to suffer from that policy of pin pricks, which is naturally also directed against the proletariat in its economic conflicts.

*But these are merely "the lttle wee ones" of its tricks.* Militarism is not content with taking part in its tenacious and dashing manner in the intricate political guerilla warfare of every day; it has infinitely higher aspirations. It knows itself to be the most important and strongest pillar of throne and altar in all the great and greatest, severe and severest conflicts of capitalist reaction against the revolution, and it has thrown its weight into the scales in all the previous great revolutionary movements. Brief references will suffice. We have already referred to the frightful laurels earned by capitalist militarism in its battles with the Parisian proletariat in the month of July, 1830, in June, 1848, and in the month of May, 1871. We have also mentioned the provocation to riot, staged by "Napoleon the Little," on December 2, 1852. The butchering of Chartists at Newport and Birmingham in 1839, when 10 people were killed and 50 wounded, deserves our special interest because it happened in England — *"Et tu, Brute!"* For two years Russia has been under military law of varying degrees of severity and given up, for the protection of the Czar's barbaric rule of the knout and the cruel suppression of the movement for liberty, to the fists, whips, sa. lores, rifles and guns of the brutal soldiery that is about to turn that unhappy country into a great cemetery, and it is only the growing revolutionary development and the corresponding disintegration of the army (which necessarily keeps pace with the energy of the revolutionary forces) that make it certain that such a "Christian," but also suicidal project will not be realized. However, Russia can be considered only with great qualifications in an examination of the capitalist countries, as has been stated several times before.

Of importance is the part played by the standing army in the first great Belgian suffrage fight and that played by the civic guard, that specifically militaristic class-struggle organization of the bourgeoisie, in the second great Belgian suffrage fight in 1902.

Apart from the calling-out of troops against the workmen who demonstrated in the Vienna Prater on May 1, 1896, and the events of Prague, Vienna and Glatz (1897), of Lemberg and Trieste (1902) which were treated of before, Austria has furnished another notable brilliant example of militaristic political action on a large scale in the electoral struggle of 1905. It is generally known that Bohemia was on the point of becoming the scene of civil war. On November 5 and 28, 1905, when the suffrage demonstrations took place, the city of Prague (where the miners were on strike, too) was filled with and surrounded by troops; the heights in the neighborhood of the city were occupied by artillery, ready to fire, some 80 persons were wounded — by the police, it is true.

The Italian events that should find a place here have already been mentioned elsewhere.

Let us now pass on to Germany whose supreme war-lord in a sentence of universal fame, which has been admitted as the most effective of weapons to the arsenal of the anti-militarist propaganda of all countries, supplied the soldiers with such a peculiar interpretation of the fourth commandment, and who not only made that well-known speech against that "rabble of men" (he meant the Socialists) at the guards' banquet, on the occasion of the anniversary of the battle of Sedan in 1895, but also directed, on March 28, 1901, that famous appeal to his Alexandrian regiment. The military preparations and the exploits of General Wrangel by which, in 1848 and 1849, the German revolutionary movement, three-quarters betrayed and entirely left in the lurch by the bourgeoisie, was overwhelmed and basely robbed of its birth right, were meant for the proletariat as such, as being then the only sound pillar of the "constitution", We further remind the reader of the Boyen-Lotzen chain affair of September, 1870, and the ravings of Bismarck and Puttkamer in which those gentlemen of the nineteenth century, at the time of the shameful anti-socialist law, anticipated and longed for an opportunity when the working people, driven to revolution, could be sabred, shot and shelled to pieces in the dashing, correct, sportsmanlike military fashion. (70) The military consignations during May-day demonstrations (71) and Reichstag elections remain very well-known up to these days, very well-known are also the incidents accompanying the suffrage theft committed against the Saxon people in 1896, and the part the military played in the "pacification" of the Saxon populace in 1896 and 1906. During the Hamburg election parades in November, 1905, on "Red Wednesday," the military, which consists of Hamburgers, was kept in the background; the sabre and revolver of the police sufficed, the result of their work were the two corpses which decorated the streets of the free Hansa city.

However, it was the 21st day of January, 1906, which showed the bulwark of capitalism in its full splendor. He who on that day, in the quiet of "holy" sabbath, saw the guns that were rattling along in the streets of Berlin might have looked into the very heart of militarism. That rattling of cannons still rings in our ears and encourages us to proceed with our fight against militarism with indefatigable persistence and unsparing ruthlessness.

On January 21, 1906, the military interference was brought about by a demonstration against the infamous Prussian franchise. We know, however, that our militarism will be just as ready to slash and shoot if the issue were the overthrow of the imperial constitution in the reactionary interest by a *coup d'état*. The latest disclosures of Hohenlohe and Delbrück have shown that Bismarck, in 1890, was on the point of dispersing the Reichstag, doing away with the Reichstag suffrage, driving the proletarian masses into the street in front of the mouths of rifles and cannon, smashing the defenceless ranks of the people to crush the Social Democracy, so as to erect with blood and iron on the lacerated proletarian bodies a stronghold of Bismarckian and junker reaction. We have also heard that the German Emperor could not be had for that plan because he wanted first "to redress the legitimate grievances of the workmen, and wanted at least to see everything done to fulfil their legitimate demands." We know that the views of the workmen and the ruling classes as to what demands of the workers are legitimate are entirely different, that the hostility shown to the Reichstag suffrage (to the most vehement opponents of which also belonged the ex-communist Miquel, as the Hohenlohe memoirs have disclosed) is continually gathering in strength at least in very influential North German circles, and that thus the danger of a "military solution" of the social question by rifle and cannon appears to be nearer than ever to-day. Should the chief of the general staff, Helmut von Moltke, be appointed Chancellor, as was recently reported, it would signify to all appearances a victory of the notorious military court party.(72)

There has never been in the world's history a lack of "grape-shot princes," (73) grape-shot junkers and grape-shot generals. One ought to be prepared for everything. There is no time to be lost.

## VETERANS' ASSOCIATION IN THE POLITICAL STRUGGLE.

It is clear to everybody that the veterans' associations are very intensely engaged in political activities, but the German Justitia has not yet been able to see it through the bandage that covers her eyes. Everybody knows, too, how they are mobilized at elections and how they force their members to leave the political organizations of the opposition. Mention must be made of their "loyal" practice of trying to prevent the class-conscious workers from renting halls for meetings. Two facts of recent date should be especially noted, viz., the boycott resolved upon (October, 1906) by the "Association of Former Soldiers of the Sixteenth Army Corps of Duisburg-Beek" against the Kaiserhof Hotel at Duisburg for having let its hall for a miners' meeting, and the expulsion from Saxon veterans' associations of proprietors of saloons and halls who rent their rooms to labor organizations. In the smaller places such fighting methods are of no little efficacy; employed against well organized workmen they are useless, however.

## MILITARISM, A MENACE TO PEACE.

International political strains can even today be produced by nationalistic antagonistic principles; by the necessity of national expansion in consequence of the increase in population, by the necessity of annexing territories with natural resources for the purpose of increasing the national wealth (i.e., the wealth of the ruling classes) and rendering the state as self-dependent as possible in point of production (a natural complementary tendency arising from the policy of protection, a tendency which, however, can be only of the slightest importance in face of the international division of labor which is establishing itself ever more vigorously and widely), by the necessity of facilitating traffic in the interior or with foreign countries (for instance, by acquiring navigable rivers, sea ports, etc.), traffic being the means by which the metabolism of the economic body, trade, is carried on; by antagonisms arising from a difference in general civilization, particularly also differences in the stage of political development. But the most important political strains that can nowadays lead to warlike complications arise, as has been already stated above, through the competition of the various countries in the economic field, through the world trade, world politics with all its complications, especially colonization. The persons on whose account those strains chiefly arise are the powerful expansionist capitalists of industry and commerce, who may be said to have an interest in a *successful* war.

It must, however, be admitted that the existence of the standing armies, which represent militarism in its most pronounced form, is in itself a menace to international peace, an independent danger of war. That is true even if we leave out of account the argument that the increase of military burdens, that Archimedean screw, can produce in a country a disposition not to let a favorable moment of military superiority pass unused, or to bring about a military decision which is thought to be necessary in any case, before any further unfavorable movement in the relative military strength has taken place. Such a disposition, as is l~nown, was not without influence in France during the latest Morocco conflict, but it is always more decisive for the moment at which the war breaks out than for the outbreak itself. But the standing army produces, as does indeed on a much smaller scale also the militia, a modern caste of warriors, a caste of persons who have been trained for war from infancy, as it were, a privileged caste of *conquistadores* that seeks adventure and promotion in war. To these must be added the groups that feather their particular nests during a war — the manufacturers of and traders in arms, munitions, warships, horses, material for equipment and clothing, provisions and means of transportation, in short, the army contractors, who exist of course also, but in smaller numbers, in countries having a militia. Both the groups who have a specific interest in war, in the making of war, viz., the officers who love adventure and the army contractors whose interest is quite independent of the *success* of the war, are composed of people of consequence. They are related to the highest functionaries of the state, they have great influence with the men with whom rests the formal decision about war and peace. They let no opportunity go by without trying to convert that influence (which in most cases they have acquired only through the exploitation of militarism) into gleaming gold, sacrificing hecatombs of proletarians on the altar of their profit. In the role of colonial enthusiasts they push the "beloved fatherland" into dangerous, costly adventures which prove exceedingly profitable for themselves, only to save that same fatherland afterwards at other people's expense in the role of naval enthusiasts in a manner which brings to them again exceedingly great profits.

The fight against the standing armies and the jingoist militaristic spirit is a fight against the danger threatening the peace of the nations. The old adage, *"Si vis pacem, para bellum,"* may be true for the individual state surrounded by militaristic states, but it is in no wise true for the capitalist countries taken collectively, with which the international propaganda of the Social Democracy is concerned. Still less does that adage prove the necessity of preparing for war in the particular form of the standing army, to which on the contrary exactly the opposite aphorism applies — *"Si vis bellum para pacem"*: there is no greater danger of war than such a peace insurance! It is true that for the aggressive economic-political imperialism of our days the standing army is the suitable form of war preparations.

As truly as the maintenance of international peace is in the interest of the international proletariat and beyond that in the interest of the civilization of the whole of humanity, as truly is the struggle against militarism — that epitome of national hatreds, that sum and extract of all peace disturbing tendencies of capitalism, in short, that serious danger of world war — a fight for civilization which the proletariat is proud to wage, which it must wage in its very own interest and which to wage no other class as such (leaving out of account some well-intentioned enthusiasts who only prove the rule) is even remotely so much interested in.

But militarism also disturbs the *national peace,* not only by the brutalizing effect it has upon the people, the heavy economic burdens it imposes upon the people and the pressure of taxes and tariff thus brought about; not only by the corruption accompanying it (see the cases of Wörmann, Fischer, von Tippelskirch, Podbielski and friends), not only by dividing into two castes a people already sufficiently oppressed by class-division; not only by its practice of maltreating soldiers and its system of dispensing justice: but above all by being a powerful obstacle in the way of every kind of progress, by being an ingenious and highly efficient instrument for closing by force the valve of the social steam-boiler. He who believes that the progress of humanity is inevitable must see in the existence of militarism the most important obstacle in the way of a peaceful and continuous evolution, to him an unbroken militarism must mean the necessity of a blood-red dawn of the capitalist idols — a capitalist "Gotzendammerung." (74)

## THE OBSTACLES OF THE PROLETARIAN REVOLUTION.

To do away with militarism or to weaken it as much as possible is thus a question of vital importance in waging the struggle for political emancipation, the form and manner of which militarism debases in a sense, therefore influencing their character in a decisive fashion. It is all the more a vital question as the superiority of the army to the unarmed people, the proletariat, is far greater to-day than it was ever before on account of the highly developed military arts and strategy, the enormous size of the armies, the unfavorable local distribution of the various classes and the relative economic strength of proletariat and bourgeoisie .which shows the proletariat in a particularly disadvantageous position, wherefore alone a future proletarian revolution will be far more difficult than any revolution that has taken place hitherto. It is important always to remember that in the bourgeois revolution the driving force, the revolutionary bourgeoisie, was the dominant economic class long before the revolution in the narrower sense broke out; that the bourgeoisie found a numerous class, economically dependent on it and subject to its political influence, which it could send into the fire and make a catspaw of, that the bourgeoisie had bought up, as it were, the old junk of feudalism before smashing and throwing it on the dumping heap, whereas all that the bourgeois have acquired by wealth the proletarians have to conquer by hunger and with their bare bodies.

FOOTNOTES

Chapter One

1. "In the social production of their life men enter certain necessary economic relations which are independent of their will, conditions of productions corresponding to a certain stage of the development of their material forces of production." MARX.

2. To the arms, properly speaking, to munition and defensive implements of all kinds, including lighting arrangements, to fortresses and war vessels, are added, for instance, the military means of communication (horses, wagons, bicycles, construction of roads and bridges, inland navigation, railroads, automobiles, telegraphy, wireless telegraphy, telephones), not forgetting the telescope, air-ships, photography and war dogs.

3. The Italian development in the XVth century is also of the greatest interest in this connection and allures the investigator into absorbing studies. It confirms throughout our fundamental conception. Cf. Burckhardt, "Kultur der Renaissance in Italien," 9th edition.

4. This also applies to the Russian revolution (of 1905) in first stage. A characteristic instance, among innumerable others, is the armed rising in Moscow in December, 1905, the astonishing tenacity of which finds an explanation in the cooperation of the mass of the urban population with the fighting revolutionaries who, by the way, were not numerous. The tactics of the urban guerilla method, splendidly developed in Moscow, will be epochal.

5. The working together in factories, etc., and the living together in the "working-class neighborhood" have however to be taken into account.

6. Cf. Burckhardt, I, p. 22.

7. Resolutions adopted at a conference of German princes and their representatives at Carlsbad, in 1819. These resolutions concerned stringent police measures against the so-called demagogues, especially professors and students who had the temerity to remind the German princes of their promises to grant constitutions to their peoples, promises made when the princes were in great trouble. Those police persecutions lasted for a whole generation and found innumerable victims among the democratic elements of Germany.

The period is generally described as the demagogue chase. — TRANSLATOR.

8. Metternich, the Austrian statesman, was the head of German and European reaction. This evil genius of Germany dominated the affairs of Germany until 1848, when he tremblingly fled to London before the infuriated people of Vienna. — TRANSLATOR.

## Chapter Two

9. Bernstein [the prominent German Socialist leader] wrongly stated in *Vie socialiste* of June 5, 1905, that modern military institutions were only the heritage of the more or less feudal monarchy.

10. One need only consider Russia where, however, entirely peculiar circumstances which did not arise from interior conditions helped to bring about the result. Standing armies resting on a basis different from that of universal military service are, for instance, the mercenary armies. In the Italian cities of the XVth century militias were also known (Burckhardt, p. 327).

11. In his well-known letter to Bluntschli (December, 1880) we read: "Eternal peace is a dream, and not even a beautiful one, and war is a part of God's world order. In it are developed the noblest virtues of man, courage and abnegation, dutifulness and self-sacrifice at the risk of life. Without war the world would sink into materialism." A few months earlier Moltke had written: "Every war is a national misfortune" (Collected Works V, p. 193 and p. 200), and in 1841 he even wrote in an article that appeared in the *Augsburger Allgemeine Zeitung*: "We confess openly to be in favor of the much derided idea of a general European peace."

12. The value of the entire foreign trade of the world rose, according to Hubler's tables, from 75,224 million marks in 1891 to 109,000 million marks in 1905.

13. "What complicates our situation to-day and renders it more difficult are our oversea pursuits and interests."

14. Moltke's views in this respect were highly fantastic. According to him the times when wars were resolved upon by cabinets were indeed past, but he considers the *political party leaders* to be wicked and dangerous provokers of war. The party leaders and — the stock exchange! It is true that here and there he has a deeper view of things (Collected Works, 3, pp. I, 126, 135, 138).

15. Characterized by that fantastic abortion, entitled, "The Invasion of 1910."

16. On account of the quarrel about Morocco France spent, in 1906, far more than a hundred million for the military protection of her eastern frontiers.

17. About the alleged, not yet fully explained plan of Semler, the Reichstag representative of the Hamburg shipowners, to capture Fernando Po in the Jameson manner, see the budgetary debates of the Reichstag of December, 1906.

18. That is not disproved because he declared for the time being against universal military service, which is regretted by the *Kreuzzeitung* [the junker organ], of November 29, 1906, because, according to the paper, universal service would educate the English people into a better understanding of the seriousness of war. In *Germany*, of course, universal military service has only the importance to force the people to make sacrifices in blood and money, in conformity with the will of the noble knights of the *Kreuzeitung*, whilst the decision about peace and war rests with those for whom the seriousness of war exists least. They can even appreciate democracy for *abroad*! Concerning the strong tendency in England and America towards a universal militia.

19. Cf. Roosevelt's message of December 4, 1906.

20. Chiefly motivated by the Morocco conflict.

21. Twenty-four and three-fourths millions for the navy, 51 millions for the army, 7 millions for interest — a total increase of some 83 million marks as compared with the budget of 1906-7. Fine prospects of further extravagant naval armaments were held out by an evidently inspired article that appeared in the *Reichbote*, on December 21, 1906. To all that must be added the enormous expenses for colonial wars (454 millions for the China Expedition, 490 millions already for the rebellion in Southwest Africa, 2 millions for the rebellion in East Africa, etc.); the question of footing those bills led, in December, 1906, to a conflict and the dissolution of the Reichstag.

22. See *Berliner Tageblatt* of October 27, 1906. Note above all the notorious resolution handed in by Ablass, December 13, 1906, and the Liberal platform for the Reichstag elections of January 25, 1907.

23. *La Revue,* October 1, 1900. The "actual results achieved" by the movement for disarmament, are a well preserved secret of the editorial board of the *Revue.*

24. Germany's colonial expenditure is in a greatly preponderating measure of a military nature, even according to Dernburg's memorial of October, 1906, in spite of all his cooking of accounts.

25. Since December 31, 1900, France possesses a real colonial army which has brought her the saddest disappointments. See the *Hamburg Correspondent,* December 7, 1906 (No. 621), also note 18 on next page. In Germany they are busily engaged in creating a colonial army. We are approaching it at the double quick.

26. See Péroz, *France et Japon en Indochine, Fanin, l'armée coloniale;* E. Reclus, in his *Patriotisme et Colonisation;* Däumig, *Schlachtopfer des Militarismus,* in *Neue Zeit,* vol. 99/00, p. 365, about the *bataillons d'Afrique,* p. 369. Regarding Germany see the speech of Roeren, member of the Reichstag, of December 3, 1906, Reichstag debates.

27. Military punishment, too, here adopts a peculiarly brutal form. About France's foreign legion and *bataillons d'Afrique* see Däumig, cited above; about the abolition of the "biribiri, p. 53

28. This hypocritical and, at the same time, shamefaced excuse is now being dropped with frank cynicism; see the article, signed by G B., in the monthly magazine, *Die deutschen Kolonien* (October, 1906), and the remark made by Strantz at the pan-German convention (September, 1906), where he said: "In the colonies we don't want to convert people into Christians; they are to work for us. This humanitarian softheadedness is downright ridiculous. German sentimentality has deprived us of a man like Peters." Again, Heinrich Hartert wrote in the *Tag,* December 21,1906, that it is "the duty of the missions . . . to adapt themselves to given circumstances"; but they had succeeded *"in frequently becoming a nuisance to the commercial man."* It is at this point that the principal friction arises between the German Clerical Party and the Government in regard to colonial policy, this alone explains the furious fight entered upon in December 1906, by the merchant Dernburg against the so-called collateral government of the Clerical Party. —For America the *Kreuzzetung* ( September 29, 1906) preaches: "The simple extermination of whole tribes of Indians is so inhuman and unchristian that it cannot be defended under any circumstances, *especially as it is in no way a question of existence for the Americans."* But

where it is such a question whole tribes may be "exterminated" even by the believer in Christian charity — according to the views of the colonial Christian.

29. See the memorable debates of the German Reichstag between November c8 and December 4, 1906, where the " abscess was lanced."

30. See *Hamburger Nachrichten,* November 3, I906.

31. The number of the victims of the wars between 1799 and 1904 (excluding the Russo-Japanese War) is estimated at about 15,000,000 men killed.

32. Cf. Moltke, p. 24, note 6, of this book, and "Moltke's Collected Works," II, p. 288. In his opinion war is supposed to promote virtue and efficiency, especially moral energy.

33. That task of bolstering up the existing interior order of things devolves upon militarism not only in the capitalist order of society, but in all societies based upon class-division.

34. See the struggle between the French state and church during the conflict of December, 1906.

35. See the disorders during the election in Upper Silesia in 1903.

36. Since the above was written great changes have taken place in the army system of Great Britain. During the world war the mercenary army has disappeared and a conscript army has taken its place. Moreover, in the years immediately preceding the war Great Britain's volunteer forces underwent great changes in composition and name. The militia, too, ceased to exist, either in name or in fact, after 1908. [TRANSLATOR. ]

37. In 1905-6, 229,820. In the Native States 136,837 soldiers in 1903.

38. Recruiting is becoming ever more difficult, and the percentage of alien recruits is growing, a fact that worries the American government.

40. Even Sheriff von Sievers-Roemershof writes of the "blood-thirsty Circassians" in the *Dünazeitung* of December 4, (17,) 1906.

41. Not even, as now proposed, in the modern way of jobbing away and discounting concessions and natural resources to American

trusts, that last invention and cry of despair of the financial policy of Czarism

## Chapter Three

42. A word coined in Germany to describe those parts of Prussia situated east of the river Elbe, the home of the Prussian junkers. [TRANSLATOR.]

43. "*Kadavergehorsam*" (the obedience of the corpse) is the expressive word used in the German original. [TRANSLATOR.]

44. A dangerous method from a sanitary point of view, which in France, for instance, is leading to a very extensive infection of the people with tuberculosis and syphilis. The French army shows from five to seven times more cases of tuberculosis than the German army. In a few decades, exclaims a warning voice in France, France will be decimated if the barracks system be not abolished. young men. Various means are employed for that purpose.

45. We need only point to the intentioned helplessness of the police in face of disorderly soldiers, and especially officers. The reader is further referred to the privilege of the soldiery to march in processions of unending lengths through the cities and thus to disturb traffic greatly without rhyme or reason — to satisfy, of course, the demands of military æsthetics. The acme of the ridiculous conceit of this carefully reared craziness was seen some years ago in Berlin when the fire brigade, hastening to a fire, was simply stopped by a military column that crossed its route and that felt no inclination to have its beautiful and majestic order deranged. It is true, this was condemned later on.

46. These are indeed strange saints! The reader may remember the Bilse case of the month of November, 1903, the many small garrisons" after the Forbach model, the gambling and champagne decrees, the officers' dueling practices (that *fine fleur* of the officers' honor), the stabbings of Brüsewitz and the shooting propensities of Hüssener, the Ruhstrat affair and that of the "harmless," the novels of Bilse and Beyerlein depicting the life of the officers with photographic truth, "First-class People" by Schlicht (Count Baudissin), the scandals about Jesko von Puttkamer and, last but not least, that about Prince Arenberg which also belongs to this category. The *French* "Little Garrison," Verdun, raised much dust in the fall of 1900. In the eyes of the worshippers of the uniform all these things are of course mostly considered as mere "amiable, piquant

weaknesses" of the worshipped saint, who is, however, very particular about people confessing the Christian creed. Naturally, we find here, too, that international solidarity of the noblest and best. An interesting case is the ragging practice of the officers of the English grenadier guard regiments, which were exposed at the beginning of 1903.

47. The German non-commissioned officer has been called the "representative of God on earth."

48. The most shocking proof is furnished by the statistics of suicides among soldiers. Those suicides of soldiers are another international phenomenon. According to *official* "statistics" one soldier among 3,700 committed suicide in Germany in 1901; in Austria, one among 920 In the 10th Austrian army corps 80 soldiers and 12 officers committed suicide in 1901, 127 others became insane and left as invalids in consequence of self-mutilation and maltreatment. In the same period 400 men deserted and 725 were condemned to hard labor or close arrest. In Austria, of course, the conflict of nationalities greatly contributes to aggravate the situation.

49. This premium system, with a maximum of 1000 marks was introduced for the whole of Germany in 1891, after having been in existence before that time in Saxony and Württemberg and after having had a forerunner in the empire in the "non-recurrent extra-pay." It is also met with elsewhere; in France, however, where the amounts are much higher (up to 4,000 francs), it has been employed with little success. The schools for non-commissioned officers are also a case in point.

50. The speech made by Chancellor Caprivi (Bismarck's successor) in the Reichstag, on February 27, 1891, is the classical confession of a noble capitalist-militarist soul of its troubles and anxieties, its hopes and aims and the methods adopted in the pursuit of those aims. It throws wide open a window through which we can have a good look at the most secret parts of that soul. The speech begins with the statement that the government refrained from re-introducing the expired *anti-socialist law* [by which Bismarck had sought to fight down socialism during the preceding dozen years or so — TRANSLATOR] only on the understanding that all possible measures be resorted to in order to cut the ground from under the feet of the Social Democracy and engage in a struggle with it; *one of those measures* (clearly a substitute for the anti-socialist law) was to consist of *the premiums for non-commissioned officers in conjunction with*

the *"Zivilversorgungsschein"* (a warrant entitling the holder to a place in a civil office). Caprivi continued: "The demands made on non-commissioned officers increase on account of the growing education of the nation. A superior can fill his position only if he feels superior to the men entrusted to his charge....

"The maintenance of discipline has in itself become more difficult, and it becomes harder still when we have to take up the struggle with the Social Democracy; I mean by this not the struggle by means of shooting and bayoneting. My memory goes back to the year 1848. Conditions were far better at that time, for the ideas had then not arisen through long years of propaganda; they cropped up suddenly and the old non-commissioned officers had a much easier task in dealing with the men than they have now in dealing with the Social Democracy. (Quite right! on the benches of the parties of the Right.) And, touching upon the most extreme case, we want far better non-commissioned officers in street fighting against the Social Democracy than in fighting against the enemy. When facing the enemy the troops can be filled with enthusiasm and willingness to sacrifice by means of patriotism and other lofty sentiments. Street fighting and all that is connected with it is not calculated to raise the self-reliance of the troops, who always feel that they are facing their countrymen." . .. "The non-commissioned officers can retain their ascendancy only if we seek to raise their status. The allied governments [this is the official title of the German federal government — TRANSLATOR] desire to raise the level of the class of the non-commissioned officers." He went on to say that it was necessary to create a "class of people" who were "bound to the state with every fibre of their existence."

This is likewise a fine description of the psychology of the elite troops.

51. Arrest combined with the deprivation of food, bed and light; extra-drill, etc.; the barbaric "tying up" in war-time. The Austrian practice of "binding hand and foot" and "tying up," the Belgian cachots, the international naval cat-o'-ninetails and similar devices are well known. Less well remembered are perhaps the atrocious instruments of torture employed in the French disciplinary sections, even against "political" refractory elements — the *poucettes*, the *menottes* and the *crapaudine* (see the pamphlet, *"Les bagnes militaires,"* published in 1902 by the *Fédération socialiste autonome de Cher,* a speech by Breton in the French Chamber, with illustrations; Georges Darien, "Biribiri," (the collective name of all military disciplinary

institutions in North Africa), *Dubois-Desaulle, "Sous la casagne,"* both published in Paris by Stock. Material about the *compagnies de discipline, pénitenciers* and the *travaux forces* (penal companies, penitentiaries and hard labor) in the French Foreign Legion and the victims of these institutions can be found in Däumig's article in the *Neue Zeit,* vol. 99-100, p. 365, and especially p. 369. At this writing energetic attempts are being made to suppress the "biribiri," (Debates of the French Chamber, December 8 and 10, 1906).

52. The *military* results of these educational methods are dealt with elsewhere. We must also point out their *moral* results, which induce the bourgeois, the anarchist and semianarchist opponents of militarism to let themselves be carried away by an indignation breathing an uncommon passion and delivered with a verbose pathos. "The army is the school of crime" (Anatole France); "drunkenness, sexual immorality and hypocrisy, that is what life in the barracks teaches" (Prof. Richet). According to the *"Manuel du soldat"* the time of military service is an "apprenticeship in brutality and vulgarity"; "a school of debauchery"; it leads to "moral cowardice, submission and slavish fearfulness." Indeed, one can scarcely imagine certain military festivals without the patriotic drunkenness, which is of course "upholding the state." Consult the *Leipeiger Volkszeitung,* of December I, 1906 about "the drinking and rioting festivals" of the veterans' associations (words used by Pastor César). The *sanitary* results are likewise anything but gratifying. Concerning the French army, see note 3; the sanitary state of the standing armies of England and America, those *democratic* countries, is downright terrible; the death rate is far higher in those countries than in Germany. Cf. Surgeon-General R. M. O'Reilly's report of 1906 with regard to dysentery and alcoholism.

53. We naturally include in the battle against the interior enemy the fight carried on against the spirit of international solidarity which is opposed to "militarism for abroad."

54. It should be explained that in Germany it is the ambition of most well-to-do young men to become a lieutenant of the reserve after having served in the army for one year as a volunteer. The title of lieutenant of the reserve is the key to official society. [TRANSLATOR ]

55. The bold exploit of the "captain of Koepenick" that ingenious cobbler and jail-bird, has exactly in this connection been pointed to as the writing on the wall, and that also by Liberals.

56. Colonel Gädke, when no longer in active service, had criticized the German war minister in the columns of the *Berliner Tageblatt*, a radical newspaper whose military expert he was at the time. The criticism concerned a speech in the Reichstag in which the minister had defended the duel. Gädke had to appear before a court and lost his military title. He then took the case before the imperial (federal) court and won. [TRANSLATOR.]

57. Liebknecht here refers to the former custom of making old superannuated soldiers school-teachers. [TRANSLATOR.]

58. There exists in Germany a kind of union of these officials — The Association of German Military Claimants of Civil Employment.

## Chapter Four

59. The men that reorganized the entire Prussian army system after the Prussian army had been shattered at Jena by Napoleon, in 1806. [TRANSLATOR.]

60. In Manteuffel's sensible command of April 18, 1885, we read: "Insults attack the sense of honor and kill it, and the officer who insults his subordinates undermines his own position; for there is no dependence on the loyalty or bravery of him who allows himself to be insulted." . . . "In a word — as the subordinates are treated by their superiors, from the general to the lieutenant thus they are."

61. A slight indication is furnished by the mass of deserters and men liable to military service who disobeyed orders to join the army. No less than 15,000 German deserters perished in the French colonial army during the first thirty years of the existence of the "splendid German Empire," whilst the bloody battle of Vionville in the Franco-German War resulted in only 16,000 men being killed and wounded.

62. Every soldier fighting in German Southwest Africa meant an annual expense of 9,500 marks to the German Empire in 1906

63. In France, for instance, in 1905: 1,101,260,000 francs. Since 1870 France has spent some 40 billion francs for military purposes (exclusive of the colonies).

64 "Kulturaufgaben" — a very difficult word to translate correctly. The lately much derided German word Kultur does not merely signify material civilization, but civilized life in its widest aspect. [TRANSLATOR.]

65. The practice of officers of engaging private soldiers as domestics. [TRANSLATOR]

66. See Hillquit's History of Socialism in the United States, which has been mostly used for the part referring to the United States.

67. The name of an inoffensive workman who had one of his hands hacked off by an infuriated custodian of law and order whose identity was never disclosed. [TRANSLATOR.]

68. The foot-note, continued, refers to the first great modern strike of the Westphalian miners, in 1880, when the men, who had great faith in the then very young Emperor, sent a deputation to Berlin to ask for his help. [TRANSLATOR.]

69. A great German iron-master who was notorious for his reactionary views and his patriarchial ideas on industrial life [TRANSLATOR.]

70. Ludwigshafen in the Palatinate was literally occupied by troops on the Sunday preceding the Reichstag elections of 1887, and only the self-possession of the Social Democrats prevented the rifles from going off. Of interest in this connection is an utterance by the German Emperor which is entered under December 12, 1889, in Hohenlohe's reminiscences: "then (when the Social Democrats had the majority in the Berlin city council) they would plunder the bourgeoisie; it was all one to him, he would have the castle loop-holed and watch them pillage; then the bourgeois would be forced to implore him to help them."

71 The first May-day demonstration (1890) deserves particular attention as the "military party" (Hohenlohe's reminiscences, September 14, 1893) then wanted very much to use the occasion for a bloody settlement with the troublesome and hated Social Democracy. into the very heart of militarism. That rattling of cannons still rings in our ears and encourages us to proceed with our fight against militarism with indefatigable persistence and unsparing ruthlessness.

72. This coming man is characterized by the Berlin *Tageblatt* as follows: "Helmut von Moltke is considered a pronounced reactionary, a quality tempered with a certain soldierly frankness and buoyancy, but he is also said to have spiritualistic inelinations. He is not at all a man of theory, but rather a dashing fighter who also possesses the 'courage of coolness' to carry on politics with the

slashing sabre and the shooting rifle." So here we find at last the qualities desired by our violent reactionaries all in one heap!

73. Grape-shot prince was the name given73 the Prince of Prussia, the later Emperor William I., who was the head of the military camarilla that tried to crush and finally succeeded in crushing the revolutionary movement in Germany in 1848 and 1849. [TRANSLATOR.]

74. The German title of Nietzsche's "The Twilight of the Idols." It is a titular parody on Wagner's "Götterdämmerung." [TRANSLATOR.]

Lightning Source UK Ltd.
Milton Keynes UK
UKOW04f1858020715

254530UK00001B/86/P